> This book is dedicated to the Architects and Builders who have made Worthing what it is today, together with those who seek to preserve the best for future generations.

©Judyth L Gwynne
the moral right of the author has been asserted

Published by: Judyth L Gwynne

Page layouts, production and printing:
Redsmart, Bude, Cornwall EX23 8BB

ISBN: 978-1-3999-1732-2

The author and publisher take no responsibility for any errors, omissions, or contradictions which may exist in this book.

To Maete with love Jud

June 2022

Judyth L Gwynne is also the author of
The Illustrated Dictionary of Lace (Batsford 1997)
and
The Empty Carriage (2020)

The Houses That George and William Built - Their Life & Times

FOREWORD

The author Judyth Gwynne is a valued and long-standing member of the Worthing Society. The aims of the Society are to secure the conservation of buildings of historic interest and to promote the social history of the town. We also aim to stimulate education, interest and research.

The Regency and Victorian periods of the town's heritage are very well documented but not so the years following World War I, leading up to the second World War and beyond. This book provides an important record of this period, documenting both the social and architectural history of the town. In the longer term, it will provide a valuable source of research for all those interested in Worthing's heritage. This unique and personal family record opens up a treasure trove of information about this period, filling a significant gap to broaden our 'heritage map'. The illustrations also provide an exceptional historical and photographic record of both the family and the social history of Worthing during these times. This element has been very well researched and highlights too the difficulties experienced by Worthing's population in recovering from both world wars.

The author's father, Leslie William Waterman was instrumental in this endeavour by purchasing land to build much needed housing and provide employment during these difficult times. He worked with noted Architects of the day and many of the buildings along the East Worthing seafront area bear testimony to this generous initiative. The Art Deco style Onslow Court, a landmark building, is a particular example of what was achieved. This building stands today as a reminder of the considerable architectural achievements of the family and those who worked with them.

I understand both Worthing Museum and Library and the West Sussex Records Office have asked for a copy of the book to add to their reference material. This indicates the significant value of this work in recording the historical development of Worthing. History students and the wider community will appreciate the author's meticulous work in sharing and dedicating her family's unique contribution to the people of Worthing.

The book is a tremendous tribute to the author and her family, forming a valuable legacy to this and future generations. I am honoured to have been asked to write this introduction and will be adding a copy of this important reference book to our Archive and the Worthing Society Library.

Susan Belton
Worthing Society Chairman
November 2021

The Houses That George and William Built - Their Life & Times

INTRODUCTION

Everyone dreams of that elusive crock of gold at the end of the rainbow or holding the winning Lottery Ticket, but one day on clearing out my 'office' (formerly Dining Room), I found underneath all the piles of old files, a typed manuscript. This was my Mother's Memoirs of her childhood growing up in Worthing.

I sat down and read the long foolscap pages enthralled, fascinated, and as I read, I realised I had found a gem. My Mother's famous ability for total and accurate recall of past events right into her late 90's was well-known by her family. Rob Blann (both relation and friend), has in the past put a spotlight on some of her Worthing stories in a series of articles in the West Sussex Gazette, published in the January and February 1995 editions of the newspaper. *(See copies at the back of the book, Appendix item 8, pages 113-114).*

Subsequently, I found more stories typed out on the little old portable typewriter on her dining room table, piecing together her life, particularly the dramatic pre-war era which brought some riches to her family and then, financial disaster. It is her story which I have woven into the larger picture, which features both my grandfather and father giving a more rounded picture of their life and times.

I make no apologies for telling the story of my two forebears and their part in the building of Worthing. Worthing is made up of many elements and has grown gracefully from a little fishing village to the town it is today, a quieter edition of its more lively neighbour Brighton.

PREFACE

My intention in writing this book was to highlight two very different men, one coming from one of the poorest communities, ie. fishermen, and the other, a Grammar school boy coming from a reasonably prosperous, Hertfordshire family. Fate certainly played a part in both their destinies but hard work and, in the case of Leslie William (Bill) filled with a young man's burning desire to help his fellow man, would lead them both by very different routes to riches.

By the beginning of the 20th century, new and exciting means of travel had arrived such as the motor car and from 1910, the early aeroplanes could occasionally be seen flying from Shoreham Airport. Communications in many areas were opening up particularly in the era near the end of George Edwin's life and the beginning of Bill's appearance on the scene in Worthing.

However, as can be seen on the brick fields plan[1], in the 19th century, large areas of the town were devoted to glasshouses and nurseries supplying early fruit and flowers to Covent Garden market and Brighton. There were two Vineyards, the Paramatta and Onslow Vineries, situated to the east of the town, an indication of the suitable growing conditions and mild climate. Also, as can be seen in Bill's story, to the west of the town, large fields of lavender were grown for the perfume trade.

In 1880, the fishing industry was at its height with catches such as mackerel and herring, which may well have brought the town to the attention of the third most important character in this story. It has been my pleasure to bring into the limelight, the fish wholesale merchant and philanthropist, George Jonathan Mills.

The period 1863 to late 1930's which encompasses this book and covers the active period of all three men, saw new utilities such as mains gas and electricity affecting the daily life of the inhabitants of the town. Trams and motor buses ran regular services replacing the reliance on horse and cart. The warmer climate and sea air drew many to settle in the town for their health and retirement and this factor had led both George Jonathan Mills and later, Bill's family, to put down roots in Worthing.

Footnotes
[1] As shown in the fully illustrated plan found on page 107, Appendix item 5.

The Houses That George and William Built - Their Life & Times

CONTENTS

Page	
1	Foreword
3	Introduction
4	Preface
5	Contents
6	List of Photographs & Illustrations
8	Chapter 1 - Planning
13	Chapter 2 - Health
19	Chapter 3 - 20th Century Home Economics
22	Chapter 4 - Recreation
31	Chapter 5 - Country Life in the late 19th and early 20th Century
36	Chapter 6 - Education
40	Chapter 7 - Communications and Travel
48	Chapter 8 - The Architects
63	Chapter 9 - George Jonathan Mills
72	Chapter 10 - George Edwin Steere
82	Chapter 11 - Leslie William Waterman
95	Appendix
96	*item 1* The Windsor Estate, Worthing Draft Deed modifying the Covenant 1902
102	*item 2* Family Tree
103	*item 3* List of Buildings (1936) designed by known Architects
104	*item 4* Population and Houses Graph
105	*item 5* Maps
109	*item 6* Architects and Eras
112	*item 7* Significant Dates in the Period 1853-1945
113	*item 8* Rob Blann Articles
115	*item 9* Before Clarence Court
116	*item 10* Freedom of the City of London
117	Acknowledgements
118	Index of Names

LIST OF PHOTOGRAPHS AND ILLUSTRATIONS

Fig. 1	Edward Charles Waterman on Worthing Beach	*Page 16*
Fig. 2	Photograph of actress Margaret (Maggie) Brennan	*Page 24*
Fig. 3	Dorothy with model hat	*Page 25*
Fig. 4	The Swan Inn at Fittleworth	*Page 34*
Fig. 5	George Edwin Steere with early bicycle	*Page 44*
Fig. 6	Dorothy in sidecar James 750 motorcycle	*Page 45*
Fig. 7	Late 1920's Jowett car	*Page 46*
Fig. 8	Dorothy & The Cassels off to Worthing 1922 Austin Tourer	*Page 47*
Fig. 9	Site plan of Heene Way	*Page 51*
Fig. 10	Heene Way 1936	*Page 52*
Fig. 11	Sketch of Heene Way Type 1	*Page 53*
Fig. 12	Heene Way Illustration Type 2 House	*Page 54*
Fig. 13	Heene Way Illustration Type 4 House	*Page 55*
Fig. 14	A Becket Gardens Type B 2 House	*Page 56*
Fig. 15	Mortgage Repayment plan 1930's	*Page 57*
Fig. 16	Lancaster Court, Hurst Avenue, Worthing	*Page 58*
Fig. 17	Thomas a Becket	*Page 58*
Fig. 18	Onslow Court, Brighton Road	*Page 59*
Fig. 19	Onslow Court Sales Brochure Front Cover	*Page 59*
Fig. 20	Onslow Court Sales Brochure	*Page 59*
Fig. 21	Clarence Court, Bright Road	*Page 60*
Fig. 22	Wellesley Court, Wallace Avenue	*Page 60*
Fig. 23	Downview Court	*Page 60*
Fig. 24	Colonnade House, Warwick Street	*Page 61*
Fig. 25	Brighton Road, Worthing	*Page 61*
Fig. 26	George Jonathan Mills	*Page 63*

LIST OF PHOTOGRAPHS AND ILLUSTRATIONS
(continued)

Fig. 27	Colville, 33 Gratwicke Road, Worthing	*Page 64*
Fig. 28	Letter from Aunt Dorothy Steere	*Page 65*
Fig. 29	Copy Front Cover Windsor Estate Deed Covenant 1902	*Page 66*
Fig. 30	Windsor Estate Deed of Covenant first page of Indenture	*Page 67*
Fig. 31	George Edwin Steere Portrait	*Page 72*
Fig. 32a	John Nathaniel Brice	*Page 77*
Fig. 32b	Emily with baby Jack Brice	*Page 77*
Fig. 33	John Nathaniel Brice's The Freedom of the City of London	*Page 77*
Fig. 34	Baltimore Guest House, Brighton Road	*Page 79*
Fig. 35	Windsor Hotel	*Page 80*
Fig. 36	Portrait of Leslie William Waterman	*Page 82*
Fig. 37	Edward Charles Waterman meeting the Duke of York	*Page 83*
Fig. 38	Portrait of Dorothy Grace Waterman circa 1920's	*Page 88*
Fig. 39	Apple Tree Cottage, Rectory Road	*Page 88*
Fig. 40	Apple Tree Cottage, Sitting Room	*Page 89*
Fig. 41	Apple Tree Cottage, Bedroom	*Page 89*
Fig. 42	Frank and Ada Matley 1929	*Page 90*
Fig. 43	Barclays Bank Goring Road, 1936	*Page 92*
Fig. 44	Barclays Bank Goring Road, 2020	*Page 92*

The Houses That George and William Built - Their Life & Times

Chapter 1
Planning

Recording her memories of the first few years of the 20th Century Dorothy would say...

"Worthing was a small country town - a seaside town. Everyone knew everyone else, or at least knew who they were, and what their job was, or if not a job, what their interest was, such as sailing and taking their daily pre-lunch drink at the yacht club. Mr. Strange, the owner or part owner, of the drapery store "Smith and Strange", would leave punctually to have his lunch at 10 o'clock at home. Mr. Strange was the father of two little girls, Joan and Kitty, who were friends of mine, and still are in our 80's."

At that time the 1901 Census recorded that the population had grown to nearly 24,500. The 'Fever Year' apparently had not made a significant brake on the growth of this fast-developing town *(see the Population Graph on page 104)*.

Two important Acts of Parliament were enacted when the duty on bricks and the abolition of the Window Tax occurred in the 1880's, which led to a building boom in the following years. These two factors were very much to the advantage of the young George Edwin as he launched himself out into the property market. Furthermore, the 19th century builders of Worthing were in a good position regarding the comparatively easy access to their building materials such as bricks and timber.

Timber was brought into the nearby port of Shoreham *(see Map of The*

River Adur on page 106) and as soon as the Baltic ports of Russia, Norway, Sweden and Finland were freed from their winter ice and snow, ship-loads of valuable [1]timber were delivered to this port. Included in the loads would be different types of timber such as Redwood Northern Pine, Scotch Fir, Red and Yellow Deal and Oak. Perhaps surprisingly, this last wood was also imported from America, Austria and Japan. These woods were used for good quality doors, windows, floors, roofs etc and cheaper-grade woods such as Whitewood, White Pine, European and Canadian Spruce and Douglas Fir for example, were imported from British Columbia and used for internal work such as doors, flooring and panelling.

Also situated at the nearby port of Shoreham was the long-established [2]Beeding Portland Cement Co, cement being another essential building material.

The 1898 Map *(second edition, page 107)*, shows the areas covered by brick fields in and around Worthing at that period and this remained a thriving industry until about 1910. The eventual demise of these fields was the [3]pressing need for more building land. This was the same fate that had befallen the extensive areas under glass devoted to fruit, vegetable and flower growing which were also inexorably pushed out by the rapidly expanding urban areas.

It is probably also pertinent to mention that there does seem to have been an issue regarding the brick fields and their manufacture with the brick workers having gained a bad name in the town generally. Perhaps the keeping of fires overnight during the firing of the bricks caused a public nuisance regarding smoke and other odours. The following extracts from sale particulars and [4]covenants of the time may well be influenced by the above points.

An item on the last page of the Windsor Estate Deed modifying Covenants *(see Appendix, item 1)* specifically states 'That the [5]Covenant against visible clothes or the burning of bricks or weeds shall remain unaltered.' Additionally, under the Conditions of Sale appended to the

Chapter 1 - Planning

Offington Park, Worthing, sale particulars in Item 2, 'No bricks or clay shall be burnt or anything permitted either during building operations or afterwards, to be or remain on the land which may be or grow to be an annoyance, disturbance or detriment to the adjacent property considered as a residential estate'.

The writer has been unable to ascertain the reason for these covenants but can only assume that, despite there being brick fields operating in the area, the builders were perhaps in the habit of making small quantities of specially sized bricks for a particular build. This is just a theory but perhaps in the absence of any other evidence on the subject it may be considered a possible explanation. However, it was not unusual for bricks to be made on site for a specific build, as was the case when the new Water Works was built at Little High Street during the period 1852-1857 using clay found locally.

Transport of heavy materials was considerably eased by the opening of the train station at Worthing in 1889 and its connections which soon followed with Portsmouth, Chichester, Bognor (Regis), Shoreham and Brighton. But of course, the goods still had to be transported from the railway depot to the appropriate builders-yard or site. By the early part of the 20th century steam lorries or wagons were available but it is very probable that in many cases the horse and cart were still in daily use as they had been for centuries.

Situated as Worthing was, with direct access to the sea, sand and gravel were in plentiful supply, but both materials had to be well-washed before they were used in the making of cement. A tragic result in using unwashed (or even partially washed) materials would, and did, result in the collapse of ceilings and walls with the resultant loss of life.

There does not seem to have been a general issue regarding the supply of labour at this time, particularly in the case of George Edwin who had been well trained by his employer, Mr. Blaker, so it would not have been necessary for him to employ other skilled labour. However, economic forces always could, and did, impel large teams of men to travel to areas

Chapter 1 - Planning

in search of work, some quite far from their own homes. This can be seen in the late 1920's when Dorothy, in her Memoirs, tells of the men coming from [6]Rochdale to build Bill's first two cottages, 'Apple Tree Cottage' and 'Chantry Cottage' with the men camping in adjoining fields during the period of the build.

The Housing and Town Planning Act of 1909 was a direct result of the publication in 1898 of Sir Ebenezer Howard's book, 'Tomorrow a Peaceful Path to Real Reform' which was re-issued in 1902 under the new title 'Garden Cities of To-Morrow'. It is certain that town planning needed to be brought under some sort of control; the writer remembers as a child in the 1930's the ugly rows and rows of large advertising hoardings at the approaches to major towns, thankfully no longer present today. However, more importantly, and referring to an earlier age, the Victorian insanitary, and squalid back-to-back houses would no longer be permitted to be built, a direct result of this Act.

Although far from Sir Ebenezer Howard's very extensive, and it might be said ambitious, schemes which envisaged an area of 6,000 acres with a possible 32,000 people living and working there, the idea that houses should be built in a more natural environment embracing nature and the countryside around certainly took hold. This can be seen in the philanthropic building of villages and Estates such as those erected by Titus Salt at Saltaire, William Lever at Port Sunlight, and George Cadbury at Bournville in 1898. Many of their Architects were undoubtedly influenced by the Garden City Movement.

In the 1920's Worthing saw its own first such development which had been originally proposed at Offington Park, just prior to the Great War of 1914-18, which described itself in their Sales Brochure as a Garden City. However, despite a resumption of this ambitious project post this war there seems to have been little appetite to purchase lots for private dwellings. Finally, the whole Estate was sold off to a land speculator who, on the same day of the sale in the early 1920's, as the surprised young Bill mentions in his Memoirs, sat down in the Auctioneers office and parcelled each section for immediate re-sale.

Nearby Hassocks had its own Sussex Garden Village and so it can be seen that the influence of this movement was affecting all the foremost Architects of the period. Bill, a country man at heart, was always mindful when undertaking a new development that natural features should be retained wherever possible, including significant well-established trees such as Oak, Elm and Conifers. Bill also instructed his Architects to provide varying designs for each development, giving an individual, almost village feel and look to their overall architectural layout. This can be seen in the development at Heene Way *(see illustrations in Chapter 8 The Architects)*.

Footnotes
[1] The source for information regarding timbers see W B McKay 'Building Construction' in four volumes, 1963.
[2] This company had been established in 1878 and was still in operation until 1991 when it was closed mainly due to environmental issues.
[3] As can be seen from Dorothy's reference to her school's 'War Work' in which the children were set to work making paper spills to support the blooms being sent to market, so it is evident, despite the war, this industry was still struggling to survive in that period *(see Chapter 6, Education pages 36-39)*.
[4] This Covenant also appears in other documents of the time, including in the Conditions of Sale appertaining to the sale of the plots in Heene Way when it states under item 4b 'No bricks shall be burnt or any chalk gravel sand clay or soil removed.'
[5] Source 'The English Semi-Detached House' by Finn Jensen.
[6] During the building of the large holiday bungalow, 'Sundial' in Old Salts Farm Lane, Lancing, for Sir James Cassels, Italian workers were employed to lay the red composite floor in the sitting-dining room. Dorothy mentions this in Chapter 4.

The Houses That George and William Built - Their Life & Times

Chapter 2
Health

In some respects, the subject of health was taken very seriously with the Spas at Bath, Buxton and Tunbridge Wells among others, catering to those suffering from a wide range of illnesses, frequently caused by overeating and drinking in some sections of society. It is clear from documents of the time, that for more serious diseases such as tuberculosis and leprosy for example, there was very little that science could do to alleviate these health problems. Many resorted to herbal remedies and folklore, and as mentioned in Dorothy's Memoirs, [1]her great grandmother Sarah Peirce, put her knowledge of herbs to good use. It is a good thing that she had not been born a century or two earlier when this kind of knowledge was looked on as witchcraft and she would have been either ducked in a local pond or worse.

However, by the 18th and 19th centuries science was coming to the fore and this led to more practical and scientific answers to the alleviation or perhaps, for the more fortunate cures of many ills. Maybe, to our 21st century minds, these so called 'cures' might have seemed just ridiculous or even barbaric, but some would ultimately lead to a real advance in helping the nation towards better health.

It is this new scientific approach to health in particular, and the pressing need to find some answers to public health issues, which due to the rising population in growing towns, had brought many towns' sanitary conditions to breaking point. It is this situation which was addressed in [2]Edward Cresy's report of 1850 made to the General Board of Health regarding the poor state of the sanitary conditions in the nearby town of Brighton.

During the Worthing typhoid epidemic in 1893, 1,300 people caught the disease and 188 died between May and September that year. It should be mentioned that Worthing was not the only town to suffer from long-outdated and insufficient sewage and water systems, with London's 'great stink' of 1858 and Brighton with the same problems attending a growing population.

In July 1893 the press reported the epidemic with headlines such as 'Fever Stricken Worthing, a holiday resort shut up' followed in August with headlines reading 'Desolate Worthing' and 'A Stricken Town'. No pleasure boats put out to sea, for there are no holiday makers to use them …. The hotels and lodging-houses are empty, and many escape the fever merely to find ruin staring them in the face…. The Pall Mall Gazette of 18th August reported 'There was panic in the air. Groups of persons stood here and there on the pavements talking of the fever and the water supply. Tanks filled with water from the West Worthing Waterworks were placed about the streets…. Many of the residents have fled and there are no visitors.' *(See also Dorothy's own comments on the effects of the Fever Year and how a small family took steps to stay healthy).*

"The year that [3]Freddie was born, was 'fever year' and the town was decimated. Mother told me much later that she hated taking the children out, for there was always a funeral passing. Freddie was a baby in the pram but George, a sturdy three year-old, would stand stock still and, as he saw the men in the street take off their hats, he did the same."

For her developer/builder father (George Edwin) this time must have been extremely worrying and Dorothy reports, "For a few years visitors and prospective house purchasers did not come."

The following item (at the top of the next page) is taken from the Sale Particulars of the West Worthing Estate, Sale Through Auction 1895.

Chapter 2 - Health

"The Worthing Corporation has recently reconstructed the main drainage and is providing a supply of pure water from the hills, thus rendering the town one of the healthiest in England, as evidence by the Statistical Return for 1894 when it was found that the death rate for Worthing was only 12.5 per 1,000, lower than any other first class watering place[4] in England."

Another sale took place in 1896 of 82 plots of land owned by the Warwick House Estate which can only be termed a disaster from a business point of view, when 68 plots were left unsold. The fever year of 1893 was still casting a long shadow, and it is evident that prospective purchasers were not confident enough at that time to lay out any sums of money either for investment or development purposes.

It may seem incongruous to the modern 21st century reader that this section on Health should include paragraphs devoted to the subject of sea bathing. However, in the 18th century this was a matter not to be taken lightly, in fact was a very serious matter as can be seen in the paragraphs below.

1892 Borough of Worthing bye-laws with respect to Public Bathing stated that [5]'Regulation Costume means a Garment or Combination of Garments extending from the neck to the knees, and being of thickness, material, shape and otherwise sufficient to effectually prevent indecent exposure of the person of the bather, Penalty for infringement £5.'

Despite these perhaps difficult strictures regarding dress for bathing, there had been an important earlier publication by [6]Dr Richard Russell entitled 'A Dissertation concerning the use of seawater in the diseases of the glands' the date of the book, 1753. This publication brought the health benefits of sea bathing well to the fore and the first bathing machines (or chariots as they were called at the time) were to appear on Worthing beaches by 1787. Dr Russell and others who followed, also recommended the drinking of a daily pint of sea water as part of the cure for many ailments with a strict regime of times and length of each 'dip' for each patient. These so called 'dips' were more a form of torture in which the patient was totally immersed three times daily in the very cold sea water for a recommended period of a few weeks. This regime seems more in the line of kill or cure and would not have been taken lightly by the patient.

Fig. 1 - Photo Credit: Family Archive. This picture of Edward Charles Waterman (Bill's father) enjoying a pipe on Worthing Beach illustrates perfectly how the older generation in the 1920's still regarded going to the beach as a dressing up occasion, with suit, hat and leather shoes.

On the other hand, his daughter in-law Dorothy sits tranquilly by in her light summer dress contemplating the sea where possibly her young husband Bill is bathing.

"There was a large canvas screen on this part of the almost deserted beach and this was for the convenience of men bathers to undress. In charge of this bathing place was a man called Coe. He had a small hut rather like a sentry box or a modern telephone booth. I do not know if any money changed hands, but Mr. Coe would vacate said box or hut and this was my changing room.

When I was a little older, perhaps 10 or 11, I was allowed to bathe with my friends - never alone. One small friend lived in a house right on the seafront in West Worthing, it was right next to the lifeboat house and the coast guards' house. We were given 6d. and crossed the road to hire a bathing machine. This was like the beach huts still on the beach to-day, but it was on wheels and was pulled down to the water by a large horse.

This was considered more discreet. I enjoyed it very much, but being of a frugal mind, thought the 6d. could have been saved had we undressed in my friend's house and just crossed the road in our bathing dresses and towels. By the side of this house was a small lane or footpath, and we would cut through this to Montague Street, where, most conveniently placed, was a shop run by an Italian called Cocozzer. His ice creams were wonderful and here I was first introduced to ice cream sodas. Two other much older Italians went round the streets with a barrel organ and a small monkey. The old woman was wrapped in a large red and yellow shawl and looked like a gypsy.

Another small friend, [7]Gladys, also went bathing with me. Our parents were friends. I do not think they knew of our expeditions to swim unattended by grown-ups, and certainly would have been frowned on if they knew we went to a very quiet part of the beach to undress among the tamarisk bushes growing wild on the beach. I think we knew we were breaking the rules, because Gladys made great haste to get dressed after the swim. I remember hearing her say 'I put my stocking on first and then I feel I am quite decent.'"

It was not unusual for children of delicate health to be sent to local farms and Dorothy reports that Guido Ferrari, the son of the restauranteur, would at times spend weeks on a farm at Washington (a village near Worthing) where no doubt he would have benefited from the fresh milk and eggs produced there.

It seems from Dorothy's Memoirs that it was quite normal for the younger children of the family to be sent to stay in the country for the whole summer with grandparents or other relations.

Also at that time, children were given health supplements such as 'Parishes Chemical Food', Cod Liver Oil and Malt and the thick, white Scotts Emulsion, the latter most objected to by Dorothy's brother Freddie.

Chapter 2 - Health

"On a visit to a farm at Washington in the early part of the 20th century on occasion when necessary, the farmer's wife accompanied me to the lavatory. What else can I call it? It was primitive in the extreme, an [8]earth closet. Long, smooth, clean scrubbed boards over an earth pit. Overhead was an enormous walnut tree. Strangely this primitive convenience had no unpleasant odour. It smelt of damp earth, wet leaves and that is all. It was almost like the depths of a wood in winter when the leaves are heavy and damp underfoot."

Footnotes
[1]Sarah Peirce is also mentioned in Chapter 5.
[2]Edward Cresy (1824-1870) Architect and Civil Engineer made several reports to the General Board of Health regarding the sanitation of towns, none more damning than the 1850 detailed, and to today's eyes, horrifying report on the poorest areas of Brighton.
[3]'Freddie' was Dorothy's brother Frederick Brice Steere and the George referred to was his elder brother George Edwin Steere.
[4]In fact the new Worthing Waterworks was completed in 1857 and a new outfall sewer constructed at Seamills Bridge, East Worthing was finally opened in 1897.
[5]It is to be hoped that the wearers of this cumbersome costume did not suffer as the wearers of the all-wool costumes worn in the 1930's and 40's. Embarrassed swimmers were soon clutching their water-logged garments to prevent them revealing more of their bodies than they had intended! No wonder the early costumes had lead weights placed in the hems of their garments to save any embarrassing disclosures.
[6]The full title of Dr Richard Russell's 1750 Treatise was entitled 'A dissertation on the use of seawater in the diseases of the glands, particularly scurvy, jaundice, King's Evil, Leprosy and the glandular consumptions'.
[7]Gladys was the daughter of Worthing hotelier, Horace Symond.
[8]Earth Closets were still in use right up to 1927 and beyond when it was not unknown for the sale particulars of a cottage in Goring-by-Sea, for example, to state that there was only an outside earth closet and pump water available. However, despite this lack of other modern utilities, Gas mains were laid at this particular property.

The Houses That George and William Built - Their Life & Times

Chapter 3
19th and 20th Century Home Economics

"Economy was practised in the home and underclothes for myself and my mother would be made at home, also pyjamas for my two brothers and nightshirts for my father. These garments would be sewn on an old treadle sewing machine. There were no electric sewing machines in those days.

When the boys had first gone to school, mother, a very skilled needlewoman and dressmaker, had started to make their jackets and knickerbockers and was faced with a solid male rebellion. They were taken to the tailor. This particular style of clothing was still worn years after for cycling and later developed into the 'plus fours' for golf."

Of course, it was not only making many simple, and perhaps to present day eyes, not so simple, items of clothing for all the family, but the whole family would be involved in harvesting as much as possible of the wild fruit and nuts that grew around them at the foot of the Downs. The industrious housewife would preserve these free gleanings for the ensuing winter months as Dorothy goes on to tells us...

"Berries would be picked, both raspberries and, in the autumn, blackberries and hazel nuts. In September on heavy dew mornings, mushrooms would be found growing in the 'fairy rings'. These were dark green perfectly circular areas clearly seen among the lighter, short fine hill turf. The mushrooms tasted wonderful. Quite superior to the cultivated ones now to be bought in all supermarkets.

Our collection of berries would be turned into [1]jam for the winter store cupboard. During one expedition we came across a crab apple tree laden with ripe apples. A basket of this gleaning gave us some clear scarlet crab-apple jelly.

Food was plentiful, but seasonal and mostly plain. Apples and currant bushes were in the garden and the Morello cherry trees were covered with old net curtains when the fruit was set. Birds would descend on the ripe fruit and strip the trees. Vegetables were from another part of the garden and were always fresh. There were no refrigerators and food would be kept and used from a walk-in larder with wooden shelves and perforated zinc at the window. The shelves would be covered with homemade jam and jellies."

"During the 1914-18 War it was also possible to bottle fruit in sugar Syrup. The tops would be sealed with melted paraffin wax. I do not remember Kilner jars or other purpose made jars at this time.

The running of even this modest household was a very exacting task, one which my mother must have found very tiring. She had some help with the cleaning and washing.

On wash day the fire in the copper in the scullery would be lit. This supplied hot water and white clothes, sheets, pillow cases, towels and other linen or cotton articles would be boiled. A young girl called 'Nellie' helped with this particular job. Nellie was rather backward mentally, but was a good worker and took some pride in earning a little money. Nellie would handle the heavy wet linen, put it through the large mangle with big heavy wooden rollers, and peg the wet clothes out to dry."

Dorothy tells us in her Memoirs how she and her friend, Nielia Harrison would arrive home after skating at the [2]'Kursall' roller-skating rink with their white clothes very dirty due to the dust coming from the black lead surface. Dorothy reports that the girls were surprised, and no doubt relieved, not to be scolded for the state of their clothes, perhaps they were easier to clean than they had imagined!

"To help with the house cleaning a middle-aged widow, Mrs. Baker, would come once, and sometimes twice, a week to sweep and polish. My mother was not really robust and would have been unable to cope with this by herself".

This chapter cannot be closed without recording the horrors of the annual Spring Clean when my Father would disappear for the whole week and the dogs take an exceedingly low profile, probably swiftly following Father out of the door. All this activity was very necessary in the days when open coal fires were in frequent use and the resultant dust and smoke had stained every surface. First in order would be the taking down of the heavy, usually velvet, curtains which not only adorned the windows but also hung from each major door into the Dining and Drawing Rooms. Of course, the net curtains had received frequent washing throughout the year, particularly if the house was situated in London or other city. Extra help was needed to roll up the heavy carpets and, weather permitting, unrolled on the lawn to be shampooed and eventually returned to their original rooms. However, the careful housewife would ensure that the large carpets would be turned to allow for even wear. Needless to say, any but the most minimal activity regarding meals was suspended in the Kitchen which, with all its attendant offices such as Larder etc., would be turned out with scrubbed shelves and clean paper placed on each one ready to receive the preserves of the Autumn harvests. Like a successful general after a week-long campaign, my Mother would survey her sparkling house, all the chimneys now swept, and windows cleaned. But, the happiest of all was Father who was allowed to return to the house where hot meals would appear once more on the table.

Footnotes
[1]Dorothy whilst still a child was taken to see jam being made in a factory during the 1914/18 War period and was to remember being told that wooden chips were being put into the fruit mixture (or was it some kind of pulped vegetable?) to represent the pips of Raspberry and Strawberry fruit.
[2]The 'Kursall' was later renamed 'The Dome'.

The Houses That George and William Built - Their Life & Times

Chapter 4
Recreation

An appetite to view the countryside had been created by artists such as John Constable (1776-1837) and William Turner (1775-1851). Particularly popular were the scenes painted by these and other well-known artists of the time. Day trips from Worthing also became possible with the advent of the South Coast railway line which had commenced in 1837 and short sea trips were taken from the newly built pier at Worthing. This was later enlarged and in 1889, a landing stage was constructed at the sea end, making more adventurous day trips possible.

The following pieces from Dorothy's Memoirs give us a glimpse into the different areas of a child's life in the first part of the 20th century. Although some recollections may not be termed 'Recreation' as such, it seemed a pity not to include these observations of a child recalling the sights and sounds around her, as she grew up in the comparatively rural part of England.

"This part of the Downs, near the golf links was the area where my father shot. I sometimes went with him and learned a lot of country lore from him.

I think he also remembered some of the old names for the vegetation and the land also. He called the round hill just before reaching Cissbury ring 'Mount Carvey'. I thought it was a word he had invented as I never heard it used by others, but quite recently I have seen it on very old maps."

Dorothy recalls a dramatic event which she witnessed while still a child when she tells us ....

"'Hold tight to my hand', said my brother Freddie, 'It's blowing a gale outside'. It was. But I have left myself and Freddie battling against the wind on the seafront after coming away from the cinema. It was a gale. The next morning, we heard that the pier had been blown away, and was just a tangled mass of iron and wooden planks. Of course, we had to go and look at the mess that the storm had made. I think most of the town had the same idea.

Our outing to the cinema was, I know, on the Saturday before Easter. I am not sure, from memory of the date - was it 1911 or 1912? [1]Records would tell.

This period of time was one when nearly all families made their own amusements. Walks and outings would be arranged. Picnics and visits in the summer, and during the winter months, amateur concerts were arranged in the 'Winter Hall'. This was a rather gloomy, barn-like building in Montague Street; Montague Street is now a pedestrian and shopping thoroughfare. Some of the diversions in the Winter Hall were the Saturday night 'Pop Concerts'. Long before the modern use of 'pop music' this term was used; the real advertised name was, of course, 'popular concerts.' These were held on some Saturday nights and were, I believe, entered by the door at the charge of one penny.

A local lady or aspiring shop assistant, or, more likely, some young member of a church choir, would render traditional or modern ballads. Songs such as 'Come Into The Garden Maude' or 'Madam, Will You Walk'. The latter with two performers. A local tenor - possibly rather adenoidal - would hopefully offer a contribution, with a discreetly directed glance at any lady performers.

I do not think any member of our family ever went to these 'pop concerts'. I think they may have been considered rough - or likely to become so. Also, we all - except me - played some instrument in varying degrees of competence.

Chapter 4 - Recreation

I think there were also 'readings' in the hall. Perhaps Dickens or other classical writers. Sometimes scenes from Shakespeare and, at certain seasons the subject would have a religious bearing. As I have already stated, we, as a family, did not attend these entertainments, but there was one exception. This was when travel talks were given, and even illustrated by magic lantern slides. One such travelogue was about Egypt. My brother Freddie took me to hear this, and I can remember it now. I was completely fascinated. I can remember being very puzzled to know how the old statues of the Pharaohs and their animal-headed Gods were not destroyed by the waters of the Nile, which the lecturer said, 'flooded the temples every year.'

My mother had a friend who had come to live nearby. She had rented one of my father's houses a few years before I was born. She was a retired actress, Margaret Brennan, (she appeared at the Adelphi Theatre, London) her personality was such that when she moved away while I was still small, [2]probably six or seven she was remembered, and I still can picture her to this day. As a child I was intrigued by her halo of snow-white hair. It was the type of springy tightly curled hair which required only a twist of the fingers and two or three tortoiseshell pins to keep it in place. Her clothes looked so elegant even to a small child, and her perfume made sitting on her lap a sensuous pleasure.

Fig. 2 - Photo Credit: by kind permission of Alamy Stock Images. Actress Margaret (Maggie) Brennan (1839?-1917).

She moved from Worthing while I was still very young, and went to live in a round of hotels, mostly in the north. My father was her executor and when she died, he brought back a box of new French kid gloves for my mother, containing pairs of white, lavender, beige and black gloves. I was most impressed.

Miss Brennan had some theatrical friends who came to Worthing nearly every year. They were a couple named Stanley and had their own theatrical company. This was a very small company rather in the category of the 'barnstormers'. The plays they put on were rather popular 'shockers', such as 'Maria - of the Red Barn' and 'Guilty Gold'. All the company had parts in every play and took parts in wildly differing and sometimes unsuitable roles. Mr. Stanley was a small man, rather rotund in the manner of [3]W C Fields. Mrs. Stanley was small and unremarkable in looks. I might liken her to a rather more refined [4]Nellie Wallace. This may sound unkind but not really so. It is only the distant memory formed by a child. Many years later I learned that Mrs. Stanley was without doubt Miss Brennan's daughter, and everything Miss Brennan owned was left to her. My father as her executor of course saw that this was done.

Fig. 3 - Photo Credit: Family Archives. Dorothy pictured with one of her model hats - the annual gift from the actress Margaret Brennan.

Chapter 4 - Recreation

My mother missed this friend when she left the town, but letters were received from time to time. Every year a hat box from Peter Robinson in Oxford Street would arrive for me. It was a present from Miss Brennan and contained a child's model hat decorated with pink silk roses. There is a picture of me still existing in which I am wearing one of my usual white dresses and holding one of these model hats by the long blue satin ribbons."

"My parents would go every year when the Stanley's company arrived to see their performance at the Theatre Royal in Bath Place. I must have been considered old enough to be taken when I was about six or seven. We saw 'Guilty Gold'. I do not remember anything of the play, but I do remember going backstage afterwards and smelling the hot grease paint and the naked gas flare lamps. This was my sole experience of 'backstage'.

When the musical comedy shows started their popular tours of the provinces, my parents went to all of them, and afterwards bought the musical scores. My mother played the piano well and my two older brothers both accompanied her on their violins. The fastidious Freddie always with his chin on a silk handkerchief between his skin and the violin. They played through the scores of 'The Merry Widow', 'The Quaker Girl', 'The Chocolate Soldier', 'The Geisha Girl', 'The Arcadians' and possibly others I have forgotten. I would have been sent to bed hours before and would drop asleep to the sound of music.

Sunday evening would be devoted to music of another kind - hymns. My father would always ask specially for 'Eternal Father Strong to Save', a hymn for 'those in peril on the sea'. This was I think a mental gesture of remembrance for his own father who was drowned at sea when my father was a [5]child of ten. On other evenings songs from the old traditional favourites would be played and sung, 'Annie Laurie', 'Coming Thro' The Rye', 'The bluebells of Scotland', 'John Peel' and many others. There were two songs on our repertoire which I have never heard in any other place or known to anyone else that I know. They were written by hand on music manuscript, but the paper was substituted by architects' blue transparent linen. The staves were ruled in by hand, and of course, all the notes also. One of these songs was 'Longshoreman Billy' and sung by a male voice. I think I can still remember the words –

I longshoreman Billy of Portsmouth Town
and a fine old skipper I be,
I worry the lubbers when they come down
to spend a few hours by the sea.
With my glass to my eye
every ship I descry
from a P. & O. Boat
to a whaler
I yarn all the while
in true nautical style
and they all think that Billy's a sailor.
chorus
But I ain't no sailor bold
and I never was upon the sea.
If I chanced to fall in
it's a fact I couldn't swim
and quickly to the bottom I should be.
So will give three hearty cheers
for the sailor a roaming free
A heave ho hauley
and a cheer for little Polly
Fo' the Queen and her ships at sea.

Sunday evenings in the winter would be spent by the fire. Toast would be made and butter and anchovy paste spread. My father would then take me on his knee and read to me. This was pre-school days and I could not read then, but I think my lifelong love of books began here. [6]We read all of Andersen's Fairy Tales, then all of Grimm's Fairy Tales, the latter illustrated with Cruikshank drawings. I thought them so horrible I refused to look at them. I have kept the book to this day as a sort of memento, complete with a hole in the cover where a live cinder fell from the fire while we were consuming the anchovy toast. Having finished the fairy tale period, we then proceeded to more robust and masculine reading. We read through all of 'Robinson Crusoe', 'The Swiss Family Robinson', 'Coral Island' and other adventure books. My mother would have retreated to another room long before the evening's readings were finished. She tried to read herself but could not concentrate with the audible competition. I thought at the time it was most odd of her not to like the stories too. Now I can realise how frustrated she felt.

I think I developed a taste for robust fiction and when I was able to read myself and had some pocket money, I would each week buy the Boy's Paper, The Magnet, The Gem and the superior 'Captain'. I suppose in a way these papers were a sort of education. The characters in these periodicals, Harry Warton, Bob Cherry, Billy Bunter and others were written by [7]Frank Richards, a nom de plume I believe, and they have become sort of classics. One of the papers had a competition for its young readers to write a story - of specified length - in the style of Frank Richards. I sent one in carefully giving my age - about 9 I think - and won 5 shillings. Another small bonus was an essay at school for us to write describing a cricket match. My effort won top marks and was read out in class.

Our family summer evenings were passed in very different manner. After a very early cup of tea, my parents and I would set out on our walks. Sometimes towards the downs and through the cornfields and sometimes down to the sea, along the promenade and through the unmade road which was to become Grand Avenue. The earth of the road was sandy and soft under foot with fallen pine needles. This stretch of road had the chauvinistic label of 'The Ladies' Mile'. I do not remember my brothers going with us on these walks, presumably they spent the time with their own friends. During our country walks I could never resist picking the wild flowers. Harebells, mauve scabious, ox eye daisies and poppies. I used to get scolded by my mother for picking these flowers and holding the wilting bunches in my hot hands, because the white juice from the poppies made a dark stain on my white dresses, and this was difficult to remove in the wash. Another favourite walk was through the

Chapter 4 - Recreation

fields to Broadwater, along Ham Road and so back to the sea. When we passed Broadwater Church, my father would tell me of the wreck of the ship 'Lalla Rouke' and the crew, all Indians I believe, buried in the Broadwater churchyard. I am not sure, but I think the 'Lalla Rouke' was the ship which carried the cargo of oranges. I am told that Worthing beach was covered with oranges, which floated unharmed from the wreck. The townspeople were disappointed to find the oranges were bitter Seville oranges, and Worthing was awash with marmalade. Our walk-through Ham Road would also remind my parents of the old name of the road which was 'Decoy Lane'. Once there had been a small lake or pond (where the rubbish tip now stands) and ducks would be shot and netted here brought in by decoys. I feel sure that this pond was originally a fish pond and was situated within the parish of Sompting.

There is a Saxon church here and a ruined chapel used long ago by the Knight Templars. Perhaps there was a Monastery or small religious community also, and the ponds were supplies of food during the winter.

Some of our long walks, or rambles, took us very much farther afield. On several occasions we took the train to Brighton. We would then wander along Brighton seafront and see all the holiday crowds and street shows and marvel at the miniature railway which ran along the beach under the cliffs. On one such walk we looked at the summer bungalows, all very flimsy construction, which had been blown by a great storm into the back water between Lancing and Shoreham. [8]The Cassels had stayed one summer holiday at one of these wrecked bungalows. After the 1914-18 War Jim had 'Sundial' built. Later I had many happy hours with [9]Ronnie and Frank. We swam and often played tennis at the courts just behind 'Sundial'. There was also one of the red composition floors which were put down by Italian workmen, in the main sitting-dining room.

Every school holiday I would be invited to Southwick for the day. [10]Aunt Kate and [11]Derek would meet me at the station and we played games and chatted. Derek was at school at Eton and was three or four years older than me. With Aunt Kate we played French cricket on the green, perhaps walked to the shops and played card and board games indoors if the weather was not good. We played Snap, Beggar Your Neighbour, Ludo, Snakes and Ladders and all the usual child's games. Derek taught me to play some game called 'Fives' which we played with small pebbles. At lunch time I was whipped upstairs by 'Aunt Kate'. Hands were washed, nails inspected and hair brushed. Always there were new ribbons to tie up my dark hair. Lunch was quite a polite meal and if I needed correcting 'Aunt Kate' would gently point out the fact."

Footnotes
[1]The date of the gale which blew the Worthing Pier down was March 1913. The first permanent cinema was opened in 1921.
[2]Dorothy's age which would have been about 4 or 5.
[3]W C Fields (1880-1946) American Comedian and Actor.
[4]Nellie Wallace (1870-1948) Glasgow born Music Hall star, Actress and Comedienne.
[5]This is one of the rare occasions when my Mother's usually very accurate memory was found to be incorrect. In fact, her father was aged 16 when his father was drowned at sea. It is quite possible that the information had been passed down to her by her father when she was a small child.
[6]The Public Library was opened in 1908 so there is no doubt Dorothy was able to indulge her life-long love of books and reading from an early age.
[7]Frank Richards was the pen name used by John Hamilton, author and creator of 'Billy Bunter'.
[8]For further Information regarding the Cassels family see picture at end of Chapter 7 - Communications *(page 40-47)*.
[9]Ronnie and Frank were the two eldest sons of Sir James Cassels and Dorothy's cousins.
[10]The Aunt Kate referred to was Kate or Katherine Carter, sister to the Charlotte Carter mentioned in Footnote 11.
[11]The Deryk (baptised Cyril) referred to in Dorothy's Memoirs was a direct descendant of the famous Victorian 'Fighting Ten' family. Whilst at Eton School, he had joined the Cadet Core and went straight into the Army and was killed in 1918. His father Montague Battye (1836-1929) was a Military Knight of Windsor. 'Monty' married Charlotte Carter a distant relation of Dorothy's. Source: see the book 'The Fighting Ten' by Evelyn Désirée Battye.

The Houses That George and William Built - Their Life & Times

Chapter 5
Country Life in The Late 19th Century and Early 20th Century

"My great grandmother [1]Peirce who lived at [2]Newich in East Sussex, must have been a person of very strong character because she has left lasting memories in those of her descendants who remember visiting her. Bertha Cassels said that as a small girl, her mother Lucy Terry took her to Newich and the old lady was walking about her garden in [3]patterns. She was very interested in her herb garden and seems to be very knowledgeable about the use of herbs, people in the village would ask her herbal cures for this or that ill. She was also a bee keeper, and the straw [4]ships in the small orchard were decorated with large black crepe bows when her husband died.

The bees were also informed verbally 'Your Master's dead. The bees will leave you if you don't tell the news' she said. This must be a reference to Great-Grandmother's second husband, who was not the father of Lucy Terry and Emily Brice. He must have been a very kindly man, because his step-grandchildren from London remember him with affection.

One of these children was my mother Emily Brice (Steere) who with three or four of her brothers was sent down to Newich and the country for the summer. [5]Step-Grandfather would meet the children at Haywards Heath Station, and drive them in his pony and trap for the few miles to Newich. If it rained, my mother said, an enormous umbrella would be opened to cover the trap and the children in it. In the orchard, the Grandmother said the children could eat any of the fallen fruit, but were not to pick any. Step-grandfather got around this by vigorously shaking the trees to let the ripe fruit fall. I think this would be between the years 1870 to 1880.

Perhaps a little earlier."

Dorothy then continues with thoughts of her father's own childhood brought up in Worthing but without the opportunities to go away on holidays....

"My father's memories were mostly of the countryside around and the sea and fishermen and the lifeboat men who manned the boat and manhandled it over runners down the beach and then rowed it to whatever craft required their assistance. The wooden groynes in the beaches were put up for sea defence to stay the erosion of the land by the sea. The 'pub' or hotel called the 'Half Brick' on the sea front at East Worthing is a permanent reminder of the sea's erosion. There used to be a row of coast guards' cottages south of this 'pub', they are now under the sea, and the rubble from the cottages is indicated by the half brick, or rubble found where the pub now is. The wooden groynes stopped the horse races which were run on the flat sands at low tide."

Dorothy felt very deeply about the loss over time of the flowers in the countryside surrounding her home town of Worthing. She was an artist and loved to paint the flowers and taught her little daughters all the botanical names of each plant and flower. It was this deep sense of loss and a time never to be recovered that she recorded in her nineties the following lament.

"A LAMENT FOR THE FLOWERS

Since writing these notes of my childhood memories, and some of other people around me, I have realised that I have always got my greatest happiness and tranquility from the countryside, and more particularly of the flowers of the countryside.

The then unspoilt downs were covered with very fine hill turf, among which grew wild thyme. Kipling has a word for it '... only the close-bit thyme, which smells like dawn in Paradise.' There were also juniper bushes here and there, and wild mignonette (reseda odorata) and purple and pyramiel orchids, trembling tolty grass rotudini folia and the scabius and harebells campanula, I have mentioned before. The hedges and small coppices were decorated with wild roses, honeysuckle and wild clematis, the latter bearing bunches of feathery white seed 'Old Man's Beard' or 'Traveller's Joy'.

A little way inland, near Washington, woods would be a blue haze of bluebells in May. One meadow in the north side of Chanctonbury would be golden with the honey sweet smell of cowslips. A mile or two farther north at Ashington, one farmer's meadows were covered with the lovely short stemmed wild daffodils. We children were allowed in to wheel our bicycles and for the fee of 6d., to pick all the daffodils we wished. On the hill, a little west of Worthing is the hill known as Highdown or 'The Miller's Grove'. Here the woods were thinned by the woodsmen having cut hazel branches to use and sell as pea and bean sticks. It would be a wonderful day spent here picking primroses and anenomes in the spring. The aim, if the weather permitted, was to pick bunches of primroses to decorate the church for Easter. Little paste pots were filled with water and the children's offerings placed all along the church window ledges. These woods, Clapham Woods, were of course private, but a blind eye was usually turned to a few little girls gathering flowers, and a keeper on his rounds would take little notice of us, except possibly to tell us to keep to the paths, and not leave bags or bottles from our picnic.

On the road to Washington village there was a long hill called 'The Bostal' which led down into the village. On these chalky edges of the road there grew masses of the yellow hypericum calycinium, (I do not know their common name). These pretty flowers, like small yellow powder puffs with their multitude of stamens, were irresistible to me, and despite my father's protests, I would scramble up the bank to gather them, getting my shoes white with chalk dust in the process. The cowslips and yellow hypericum are now lost for ever under the main Worthing to London Road and the constant roar of traffic.

Chapter 5 - Country Life in The Late 19th Century and Early 20th Century

Fig. 4 - Photo Credit: Mark Saunders - The Swan Inn at Fittleworth.

A little further afield, we would make a [6]day's expedition to Fittleworth, a village between Pulborough and Storrington to the south, under the shadow of the downs.

The Swan Inn at Fittleworth would in those days make a wonderful tea. There would be enormous plates of very thin bread spread with very thick butter. The jam and little cakes would all be made in the Inn kitchen. It was an interesting place and had been the headquarters of the West Sussex Constabulary, and on the walls of the stairs was a collection of police truncheons from the period of the Bow Street Runners to the then present day.

We left bicycles outside the Inn and walked up a lane away from the road. Here beside the river and early stream of the Arun which runs out at Littlehampton, we found the banks leading down to the water covered with foxgloves. We would gather sheaves of them, such a pleasure, but rather unwieldy on a bicycle! About a year ago, I think it was 1987 or '88, we drove here and found the lane closed for a private road leading to new houses, very expensive ones. I wonder if the foxgloves are still there!

Winter afternoons would then end for me with toast made before the fire with a special toasting tool made by my father. Instead of the usual fork, the end was like two round hands clasped together and the bread held between. It was less likely to drop the bread in the fire than the fork. There would be homemade jam and plain plum cake or occasionally a dough cake. This was a yeast cake rather like a Lardy cake, but I am sure it would not be permitted to add butter!"

Footnotes
[1] Great grandmother Peirce was Sarah Peirce (d.1884).
[2] Newich spelt also as 'Newick' on different Census forms.
[3] Dorothy has made a small typo and actually these 'straw ships' would of course refer to 'straw skips'.
[4] These patterns (or pattens) were probably made of wood and metal and were attached to the normal shoe to lift them out of wet or dirty conditions underfoot.
[5] Step grandfather's name was Henry Coley.
[6] This expedition would have taken about one and a half hours ride on their bicycles, but apparently well worth the ride!

The Houses That George and William Built - Their Life & Times

Chapter 6
Education

Dorothy grew up during the first World War, first attending [1]Steyne School and later the High School and she leaves us with some of her memories of those days in her Memoirs....

"Steyne School was very patriotically minded. Many of the children there did not go home for years. They were the children of serving officers in India, or administrative men in other distant parts of the empire. There was an empire then! The 24th May was a great day at school. It was Queen Victoria's birthday, although she had been dead for a number of years, the day was kept as Empire Day. The girls wore white dresses and the boys white shirts and dark shorts or trousers. Sports and a sort of 'display drill' were held in a field quite near the school. The field is now Beach House Gardens. It was especially for this day that we were taught the words of Elgar's 'Land of Hope and Glory', a lovely plangent tune too.

Our school collected pennies and shillings from children to buy a husky dog for [2]Captain Scott to use for his expedition to the Antarctic. I believe the dog was called 'Steyne'. Was this 1912? Poor 'Steyne', he was probably eaten by the other huskies at the end!"

It is quite relevant to make a small diversion here which will give an insight into the thinking of the more liberal and forward thinking of parents with girls at home needing education in order to be able to support themselves in the future. The Great War had certainly changed much of the thinking at this stage regarding the role of women in the workplace, with many young women having to fill formerly male roles in all sectors of the labour market. Almost gone now was the picture of the better-off young woman expected to remain at home solely to involve herself in domestic duties and maybe charitable works.

The building of the new [3]Girls' Secondary School near Broadwater just prior to the beginning of the 1914/18 World War was created very much to fulfil the new role that women would be taking in society in the future. The aim and purpose of this new school was to train girls to become teachers. The choice of the Head Mistress was inspired and I give Dorothy's own words a portrait of Miss Kate Coast.

"(She) was an outstanding woman and left a lasting influence on her pupils. She was not a graduate as the teachers under her were. She had no gown from the Universities to wear on Speech Days and other special occasions. She was tall and slim almost to thinness. Her straight brown hair was parted in the middle and drawn into a 'bun' at the neck. Her clothes were plain and usually tweed skirts with blouses, and of course no 'make up'. Put into words this picture is repressive and unlikeable, but this is not true at all. We all liked her very much, she was always so calm and fair."

It is interesting to see how progressive both of Dorothy's parents were regarding the education of their daughter and Dorothy's Memoirs continues by telling how a chance encounter with Miss Coast led them to move her from the Steyne School to this new more liberal school at Broadwater.

"My father always had an interest in new buildings and especially the new houses which were springing up in Worthing and expanding into the fields and lanes around the original town. He combined exercising and training his new dog and looking at the new houses in Bulkington Avenue.

Miss Coast had just moved into her house preparatory to starting the new term and my father seeing her in her garden stopped to chat to her. The chats must have grown to many conversations, and Miss Coast undoubtedly convinced him how necessary it was to educate the growing generation of girls to a more liberal and academic standard than the more usual one of basic 'three R's' and various accomplishments such as needlework, dancing and social graces."

Dorothy continues...

"I stayed at the [4]High School until I was 18 and was reasonably happy there. The first few years were subdued because of the war. The mid-day school lunch was adequate but very basic. The general feeling of anxiety and concern was felt because of the bad news of fathers and brothers killed or wounded in France. We were encouraged to keep a war diary of movements of our forces and of our allies. I fear my diary left very much to be desired. I could not really understand the movements of the army and navy, or of their victories or defeats. The two little Strange sisters were in the same class as me. I did not know them before as they were not at the Steyne School.

The elder of the two, [5]Joan, kept such a good diary that when I saw her a year or two ago, it must be 1980 or '79, she told me the BBC had been told of this 'child's' diary of the 1914-18 War, and had made it into a programme to be broadcast.

Our 'war work' was very trivial indeed. I do not really know if it was much use, presumably it was of some value. This was 'making spills.' These spills were used to pack the flowers grown in Worthing to be sent to Covent Garden. These would be the choice carnations and large bloomed chrysanthemums. The spills had to be of exact size and firmness. They were made of newspaper cut to size and covered with green tissue paper. They had to be firm and not loose or floppy. The ends would be bent and put to exactly fit the boxes, and the heads of the flowers rested on the spills.

Chapter 6 - Education

The school had good playing fields as it was newly built on meadows belonging to the "South Farm."

The rest of my school days were not very eventful. There was still the rather dull aftermath of the war years. There was much unemployment and in some cases poverty and despair, but not very noticeable in the then prosperous south. We went through all our school tasks, with some minor [6]desertions such as preparing and acting in school plays - usually Shakespeare. Once it was Goldsmith's 'She Stoops to Conquer' and I played Dorothy Hardcastle to Joan Strange's Mr. Hardcastle. There were always the choir concerts and carols at Christmas. After leaving the High School, my life took on a different period when I went to London. Here I saw a great deal of the Cassels, and after the [7]major operation to my head, I spent several years with them. None of us ever lost touch with Worthing, and all the summer days were spent in Worthing or Lancing."

Footnotes
[1]The Steyne School no longer exists and the buildings have become The Chatsworth Hotel.
[2]Captain Scott's ill-fated Terra Nova expedition took place between 1910 and 1913.
[3]This newly-built school was originally named the Girls Secondary School and created with the aim and purpose to train girls to become teachers.
[4]Dorothy's mother and Aunt Lucy had been able to remain at school and complete their education as Pupil Teachers.
[5]Joan Strange - 'A Child's Diary of 1914-1918 War'.
[6]Dorothy's word "desertions" is a typo instead of "diversions."
[7]Dorothy is referring to her mastoid operation and she says...
"My ear operation was in fact rather 'touch and go', for antibiotics were not then known and the Surgeon had to cut through the skull bones. Mr. Alex Gavin of Harley Street, told me afterwards that he was horrified when he cut through the bone, that pus came flowing out. Before this operation, when the terrible headaches started, the College got in touch with Bertha Cassels who came with the old policeman chauffeur, Jim Mace, and drove me back to Worthing. Mace told me much later 'we never expected to see you again, Miss'."

The Houses That George and William Built - Their Life & Times

Chapter 7
Communications and Travel

At the time of Dorothy's birth in 1902, Worthing was by then connected by train to Brighton, Chichester, Bognor, Portsmouth and London with local trams running in the town. The so-called 'Tram-O-Cars' were established in 1924 but the popular and more efficient buses of the Worthing Motor Services (now the Southdown Motor Services) are still in existence today.

1902 saw electric street lighting illuminating the main streets of the town. However, obviously from Dorothy's Memoirs they had not reached all parts of the town where the gas lamp lighters still went their nightly rounds.

No doubt the telephone, brought to the town in 1886, and the local newspaper 'The Worthing Record', established earlier in 1853, kept the population of the town well informed, but only the well-to-do would be able to afford the telephone.

Dorothy gives us a picture of Worthing town life in the early part of the 1900's and says -

"The streets were not then tarmacked but made up of crushed stones. When the stones were laid, a steamroller would be driven repeatedly over and over the surface to reduce it to some semblance of smoothness. Worthing is built on chalk, and the white dust rising from the roads would, in dry weather in the Summer, cover everything with a white film. In the summer a 'watercart' would be driven around the town to damp down the dust by spraying water. This vehicle was driven by one man sitting on a large water tank drawn by one horse. At the back there would be a large perforated tube connected to the water tank which sent out tiny jets of water along its legs. Very refreshing to stray dogs or small boys. In the residential streets, straw would be laid down in a thick cover in the event of illness of any person in the houses near the street. The straw would deaden the noise of horses' hooves or the sound of the iron shod cart wheels.

The milkman would come every morning to deliver milk at the door. This was not delivered in bottles but ladled by a very large ladle into small cans belonging to each household. This ladle was hooked over the edge of the can before proceeding to the next house. The milkman took his wares round in a hand-drawn cart. Our baker, on the contrary, had a small covered van drawn by a pony. The baker had a corner shop near and displayed his wares in a large window. Rolls and bread and beautiful sponge cakes would be spread out on glass plates on paper doilies. The sponges were very good, made correctly without fat, but eggs and sugar whipped over hot water until the mixture thickened. This method gave the finished cake a delicious sugary crisp top. At the rear of the baker's shop there was the bake house built above the stable for the pony and cover for the cart. The baker was my father's tenant and made him every day a special small loaf of Vienna bread. This was made of very fine white flour and I should not think it was really good for him. My father was inclined to put on weight!"

Although the motor car made its first appearance in the early 20th century on the streets of towns such as Worthing, they were very few and far between with only the very wealthy able to purchase this very new method of locomotion. It seems that Dr. Simpson, described below, kept to the earlier Victorian mode of travel by horse and carriage or trap. Perhaps with the condition of the roads at that time, as described by Dorothy, this would be preferable for the passengers in open carriages especially off the main roads. However, it was very important at that time and right into the mid 20th century for a Doctor to have a small expensive equipage which gave his patients confidence in the success of his medical abilities.

"Our doctor was Dr. Simpson. He had attended all our arrivals into the world. I believe my grandmother was his first patient in Worthing. The Doctor made his rounds in a dogcart drawn by a smart high stepping horse and a groom up behind in his top hat with a cockade at the side. A few times when his patients took him near our house, he would whip me up beside him and take me on the rest of his rounds. The groom would hold the horse's head and I would wait grandly in the front to await the end of the visit. The first occasion I was taken with him, I think it was near Christmas, I wore a crimson 'highwayman's' coat with two or three capes. I had a close-fitting bonnet of the same red trimmed with beaver fur. My small hands were enclosed in a small barrel-shaped beaver muff suspended round my neck by a round silk cord. I thought I was very smart perched up in the dog cart behind the shining horse. The front seat by the Dr. was comfortable and, with a rug over our knees, also warm. Once - for what reason I do not remember - I sat behind with the groom and found this very uncomfortable as the seat sloped forward to allow the person in front to lean comfortably backwards.

On a few winter afternoons, I would be collected by my mother who had been shopping in the town. We might take the horse 'bus, with straw on the floor, on the lower part of the 'bus. We would, perhaps, see the lamp lighter with a thin pole with a steel hook on the end, doing his rounds to turn on the street gas lamps.

One winter while I was still at the Steyne School, the principals of the school decided to advertise by using a small covered trap drawn by two very brisk Shetland ponies. The groom who drove was called Hawich. This Cinderella-like vehicle collected me and several other children from our houses some distance from the school. I believe the fee for this was ten shillings for the term. This ridiculous amount was, for some reason I do not understand, a token payment for their advertisement. I remember the smell of wet tarpaulin and warm fug inside this little carriage, quite delightful! I believe Hawich extracted drinks from my father, possibly other fathers too. Of course I mean the price of a drink! I wonder if the school inherited the small carriage and Shetland ponies, and indeed Hawich in settlement of a bad debt?"

The bicycle for the older girls gave them freedom to explore and adventure even although no doubt their careful mothers made sure that they were not alone on these expeditions. The writer is of the opinion that the bicycle was the most influential tool towards the eventual emancipation of women and girls.

"We would cycle there (the Washington Farm) and get covered by the white chalk dust. The farm house was not very big and situated near Washington church. The large kitchen had a big, recessed, black-leaded stove with flat areas of hob beside the fire box. A kettle and a saucepan or two would be kept simmering here.

It should be remembered that at this and earlier times the main means of travel, especially over smaller distances was to walk, and walking was also a pastime as many records show that families would take a Sunday afternoon walk, often going some distances to visit older relatives, or to go on expeditions to gather nuts, mushrooms and other wild fruits and berries in season."

Walking also was at times the only practical and affordable means of travelling great distances to obtain work especially for those with very little or no money. Such an instance, well documented, was the occasion when the whole of John Heathcote's workforce walked from Loughborough in Leicestershire to the new factory site in Tiverton, Devon, a journey of several days. Although taking place in 1816 it would not have been possible for such a journey to have been undertaken by train until at least a century later. For instance the Station at Worthing was not opened until 1889 and then with limited connections to places such as Brighton, Chichester, Portsmouth and Bognor.

Chapter 7 - Communications and Travel

"My mother had given up riding her bicycle when I was very young but I can just remember her with a long heavy cycling skirt which was protected from the wheel spokes by a lacing of thin cord from the back mudguard. She once told me that she and her sister Lucy were the first girls to cycle in Worthing."

Fig. 5 - Photo Credit: Family Archives.
George Edwin Steere with new ¹safety bicycle. Picture taken c.1890 on Worthing Seafront. Included in the picture a cyclist wearing the then fashionable cycling gear holding his earlier model bicycle, certainly a more than interested bystander in this picture!

It was in the 1930's that the writer, with her little sister Jo, would occasionally see a gentleman dressed in tweeds, probably a knickerbocker suit and a deer stalker hat riding a large tricycle on the main Washington to Worthing road. This large and very out-of-date vehicle (first made in the 1880's), proved however, to be unstable and therefore the two-wheel bicycle became the favoured mode of personal transport. Needless to say the children did not fail in trying to spot the tricycle on their journeys to and from Worthing and did in fact see the (old?) gentleman on several occasions.

Chapter 7 - Communications and Travel

Dorothy tells us that on showing an interest in her brother Freddie's [2]Indian Motor cycle which due to its condition had been re-named 'The Heap', and writes...

"I showed some interest in this polyglot machine and somewhat to my surprise, I was allowed to try it out and, still more to my surprise, he suggested I might ride it to Pulborough where I had to interview the vicar. This cleric had the key to the Church Hall and, indeed, had to give permission for the Hall to be used for my classes. He was an elderly man, most friendly and was amused to see me on The Heap and commended such a modern activity. I remember I wore a very full accordion pleated navy blue skirt and this garment was so wide, that it was perfectly proper to ride astride. I returned the vehicle still intact, to Freddie but I must confess, I did not enjoy my ride, much preferring a car."

Fig. 6 - Photo Credit: Family Archives.
Pictured above is Dorothy in the sidecar of what is thought to be a James 750 motorcycle.

At the same period when these early motorbikes appeared on the roads, the more elegant and commodious first two motor cars were occasionally seen, cars such as the following described by Dorothy.

Chapter 7 - Communications and Travel

"All arrived in a Daimler car. It was open and the two ladies were in the high seat at the back, and ³Uncle Alfred and Bertha's fiance, ⁴Jim Cassels in the front. Jim was arrayed in goggles and enormous gauntlet gloves up to his elbows. He of course was the driver. ⁵Lucy and Bertha had thin, light coloured, loose dustcoats over their dresses, and their hats were tied with filmy veils which tied under their chins and the ends floated behind in the breeze. They looked very elegant and smart in their London clothes.

Following this special visit (by Jim and Bertha) we made a return visit to see the Terrys in London. I believe the occasion was for my father and great Uncle Alfred to go to the cattle show at Smithfield. We went by train to Victoria and then a four-wheel horse cab took us to the Terry's. During this short journey another cab collided with ours and the shaft crashed through the window of our cab, just missing me. I remember being very unimpressed and wondered what all the shouting and noise was about. I was being clutched firmly to my mother's bosom."

Fig. 7 - Photo Credit: Family Archives.
Late 1920's Jowett - note the dicky at the rear occupied by Dorothy and Ada Matley with her husband Frank standing by.

Dorothy was so fortunate to be born in this era as she loved her various motor cars and was a confident and skilful driver all her life; although it has to be said that she was happy to leave the motorbikes to her elder brothers!

Fig. 8 - Photo Credit: Family Archives.
Dorothy with her cousins, James and Bertha Cassels, off to Worthing on holiday in a 1922 Austin 20 HP Tourer.

Footnotes
[1]The first modern Safety Bicycle was invented in 1885.
[2]The 'Indian' motor cycle referred to was made in Iowa, USA where the company had been manufacturing these bikes from 1897. Obviously, Freddie's bike had seen better days and may have been one of the earlier models which might have been the reason for its apparent dilapidated state!
[3]The Uncle Alfred mentioned here is Uncle Alfred Terry, Bertha's father.
[4]Sir James Dale Cassels (1877-1972) Journalist, Judge, and MP for Leyton West.
[5]The Lucy mentioned here was not Dorothy's Aunt Lucy Robinson but Bertha's mother Lucy Terry.

The Houses That George and William Built - Their Life & Times

Chapter 8
The Architects - Trends in style and rise of 'Art Deco' in 1925

My opening sentence to the Preface of this book states that I wished to highlight two very different men, but I also had another important mission and that was to bring into the light the largely forgotten names of the Architects who designed Worthing's most significant early 20th century buildings. It has only been through the discovery, 30 years after his death in 1990, of my father's collection of papers which included a large number of sale particulars. This collection of papers covers the period 1925-1936 and I have been able to uncover so much more information regarding this grey area in the town's history.

It is hoped that the residents of present-day Worthing will find these old photographs, taken by my father (around 1936), show how their street, or neighbourhood looked in those pre-war years. It is hoped too that the pages from sale particulars, some of which are reproduced here, also give a flavour of the times, with details present when the properties were first built. However, it will soon become apparent that many properties have been altered and changed to fit in with modern day living. On this subject, it is the Edwardian houses built by my grandfather, George Edwin, which apparently seem to have retained most of their original charm; with their little balconies leading from top floor windows facing the sea and the patterned tiles on the floors of the front entrance halls. It is the interiors however, which have seen the greatest alterations, with the large high-ceilinged rooms cut into two, and most disastrously, from an aesthetical point of view, the large marble fireplaces with their decorative tiled surrounds torn out and no doubt ending up in reclamation yards. This has made the elegant, well-proportioned rooms with their moulded ceilings and wide graceful doorways lose their focal points and although no doubt practical in modern terms, now lack interest.

Chapter 8 - The Architects - Trends in style and rise of 'Art Deco' in 1925

On the same topic of changes over the years, some of the houses in Brighton Road, for example with their glazed green pantile roofs, some balconies have been incorporated into the interior rooms thereby increasing their size. Probably, the most obvious and regrettable change in the exterior, is the removal of the Art Deco roof-line of the former Barclays Bank building in Goring Road, reducing the building to appear in the [1]"Brutalist" mode of Architecture *(see Fig. 44).*

All the above may seem rather negative commentary but there is much left to rejoice in and we have to thank these Architects for their vision which has left the town with its own unique combination of country town and visionary seaside appearance.

As mentioned in Chapter 10 - George Edwin Steere, he did not need the services, so far as is known, of an Architect and probably relied on the Pattern Books available at the time. Another factor was that only expensive [2]Architects, possibly from London, would be engaged by a builder and then only on prestigious projects such as Churches and Schools. However, there is no doubt that George Edwin knew very well the value and importance of Architects and saw to it that his two sons should be trained in this profession.

There is no doubt that Bill *(see Chapter 11)* also knew the importance, and in his case the necessity, of employing Architects. An early experience taught him a lesson for the future to only employ the best. In their first steps as developers, Bill and his young partner seeking an Architect to work with them, found to their dismay that the professional they first employed had made the almost fatal error of siting a chimney flue which, according to his plans, ran right through the staircase. Fortunately, a solution was found which avoided part of the house being pulled down and rebuilding it correctly. In Bill's view the house had been devalued by the remedial work that had ensued to put matters right. A further lesson was learnt when Bill himself was consulted in later years by one of his partners concerning a block of flats he was building where large damp areas were appearing around the windows and rain was coming into the rooms facing the sea via the ventilators. Bill's advice involved the complete removal of the windows and then rebuilt with slates to prevent the water getting through. He also recommended that the ventilators should be placed where possible in a sheltered position and if not possible another type would have to be installed. On further investigation Bill soon ascertained that the Architect employed on this project came from an inland city and had no local knowledge regarding coastal weather conditions, i.e. the rain did not fall straight down vertically but was blown off the sea horizontally thus entering the ventilation systems.

Subsequent to his one early unfortunate and possibly extremely expensive experience regarding the misplaced chimney flue, Bill always chose his Architects very carefully and over time developed very good working relations with them and it was one of these he took with him to the 1937 Paris Fair to purchase window fittings. The two main and, as he describes it later, sound Architects, [3]were Arthur Thomas William Goldsmith and Marcus Rainsford Fletcher.

It was part of Bill's guarantee he gave to each new owner of a finished property, that each stage of construction was 'signed off' by the Architect concerned thus ensuring quality control at every stage of the work.

The builders in the mid twentieth century set about wooing the housewife and one initiative, thought as ground breaking in these times, was the [4]measuring of the height of the housewife so that the kitchen sink would be erected at the correct height and therefore avoid those of the previous generations breaking their backs leaning over too low sinks. The shift in society in the aftermath of the 1914-18 War and the advent of electric and gas equipment in the kitchen, made for ease of function and in many cases doing away with the need to hire domestic help, a great assistance to the new 'modern' woman. This change can be clearly seen in Dorothy's Memoirs when she states that her Mother required help with cleaning and washing which encompassed the weekly boiling of household linens including heavy bed sheets (probably made of linen) and towels.

It is noticeable in the post 2nd World War era that the kitchen range, the copper for boiling household linens and a coal house situated close to the kitchen premises, are all being substituted by electric or gas stoves not solely reliant on continual servicing of coal or coke.

It will be noted that one of the central detached houses had already been sold prior to the publication of the sales brochure.

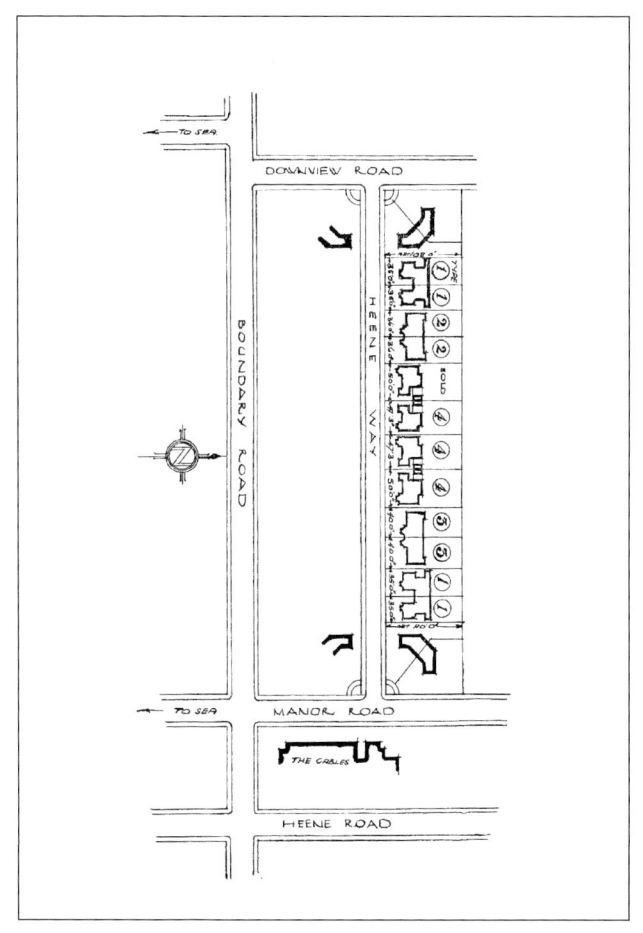

Fig. 9 -
Site Plan of Heene Way. Architect: A T W Goldsmith IRIBA (1892-1972).

Chapter 8 - The Architects - Trends in style and rise of 'Art Deco' in 1925

Fig. 10 - Photo Credit: Family Archives.
Heene Way, Worthing at 1936. Architect A T W Goldsmith (1892-1972).

The above and other 1936 photographs may be of added interest when the ugly telephone wires can now be viewed as part of the past.

Heene Way was a most desirable residential area being only five minutes from the sea and ten minutes from West Worthing Railway Station.

The 1931 Sales Prospectus relating to the building plots being offered by The Tarring Estate at the 'A Becket Gardens', contains one or two items of particular interest. The first page relates to the Type B 2 property where there has been an emphasis on the provision of a 'Separate Scullery' in the domestic offices. This might be seen as being on the cusp of the end of the old and the appearance of the 'new' as seen in the very different kitchens provided in the very up to date Onslow Court flats (built approximately 35 years later). It might be worth re-visiting the traditional domestic offices of those pre 1930 years when the ideal layout would have included, adjacent to the kitchen, a scullery for general washing up and the cleaning and preparation of fruit and vegetables, a walk-in larder probably containing a cool slab (usually slate) and also in more affluent houses a Pantry where the silver, fine glass and China were washed and stored and providing a space where special delicacies were prepared. The appearance of gas and electricity for cooking and refrigeration had removed forever the need for the coal house and later the [5]domestic copper becoming largely redundant from the 1950's with the advent of the domestic washing machine.

TYPE 1.

These Houses are situated at each end of the road (adjoining the corner properties), are semi-detached and specially planned to minimize labour. The two Reception Rooms face south, also two of the principal Bedrooms. There is no waste space, all rooms opening out of a central hall and landing.

THE ACCOMMODATION comprises:—

On the Ground Floor.

TILED PORCH.

ENTRANCE HALL fitted with radiator.

DRAWING ROOM, 14ft. plus large bay by 12ft. 6in., gas fire point, electric reading lamp point and electric power point.

DINING ROOM, 19ft. by 11ft. 6in. also with gas fire point, electric reading lamp point and electric power point. Service hatch to kitchen. French windows to garden.

Under the Stairs is a good Cupboard and behind them is the well-arranged

CLOAK ROOM & W.C., having tiled floor and white tiled dado, fitted with a first grade porcelain lavatory basin h. & c. supplies and silent flushing pedestal apparatus.

Fig. 11 - Illustration from the Heene Way Sales Brochure. Type 1 Freehold Purchase Price £1,950.

TYPE 2.

This Type adjoin TYPE 1 at the west end of Heene Way and are also semi-detached.

THE ACCOMMODATION comprises:~

On the Ground Floor.

TILED PORCH.

ENTRANCE HALL fitted radiator.

DRAWING ROOM, 14ft. plus large bay by 12ft. 6in., with gas fire point, electric reading lamp point and electric power point

Opening into the

DINING ROOM, 13ft. by 12ft. 6in., with gas fire point, electric reading lamp point and electric power point. French windows to garden.

Note.—The wall can be built up between these two rooms making them entirely separate should purchasers desire it.

Opening out of the Hall, but well screened by the staircase is a tiled floor CLOAK ROOM & W.C. with tiled dado fitted with porcelain lavatory basin, h. & c. supplies and silent flushing pedestal apparatus.

Cupboard under stairs.

Fig. 12 - Illustration from the Heene Way Sales Brochure.
Type 2 Freehold Purchase Price £2,250.
There was also Type 3 Freehold Purchase Price £2,350 which included a third reception room and a garage.

TYPE 4

TYPE 4 are Detached Residences placed in the centre of the road between TYPES 2 and 3. Particularly suitable for a family, this class of house is of exceptional value, giving larger accommodation yet remaining labour-saving and economical in upkeep.

THE ACCOMMODATION is as follows:—

On the Ground Floor.

TILED PORCH.

ENTRANCE HALL fitted with radiator and electric power point.

DRAWING ROOM, 14ft. plus large bay by 12ft. 6in. with gas fire point and electric power point.

Opening into the

DINING ROOM 13ft. by 12ft. 6in. fitted with gas fire point and electric power point. French windows to garden.

Note.—The wall between these rooms can be bricked up, making them entirely separate should a purchaser so desire.

*Fig. 13 - Illustration from the Heene Way Sales Brochure.
Type 4 Freehold Purchase Price £2,600.*

However, it is evident from the illustration below that the 1931 houses still included in their domestic offices a Scullery, Larder and Coal Store, the latter still necessary to supply the [6]open fireplaces in the main rooms.

TYPE B 2.

This Property is planned on the lines of the letter "L," thereby giving both Living Rooms a front outlook (due south to the Littlehampton Road).

The Accommodation, which is on Two Floors, comprises:—

On the Ground Floor
ENTRANCE HALL.
LOUNGE about 14ft. 6in. by 12ft.
DINING ROOM about 16ft. 9in. by 15ft.
  EXCELLENT DOMESTIC OFFICES:—
  KITCHEN fitted "Ideal" Boiler, with gas point laid on for gas cooker.
  SEPARATE SCULLERY fitted porcelain enamelled sink (h. & c. supplies) set in white tiled surround.
  Excellent LARDER.   COAL STORE.
Ample Room for Garage.

On the First Floor
FRONT BEDROOM, No. 1, about 14ft. 6in. by 12ft.
    "   "   No. 2.   "   15ft. by 11ft.
No. 3 BEDROOM, about 8ft. 9in. by 8ft. 6in.
BATHROOM fitted porcelain enamelled bath with slabbed front and lavatory basin (h. & c. supplies).
Separate W.C.   LINEN CUPBOARD.

PRICE FREEHOLD : £1,125
which includes fencing in, straightening up and part turfing gardens, also
FREE CONVEYANCE

Fig. 14 - Illustration from the Heene Way Sales Brochure. Type B 2 Architect: M R Fletcher. Freehold Purchase Price £1,125.

Appended below is the somewhat flowery description of the properties being advertised for sale:-
'It should be specially noted that all Houses are built with best quality English made bricks, cheerfully harmonizing with the open rural situation, the whole set off with leaded light windows and green paintwork.'

All these descriptive details are very much in keeping with the ethos of the Art Nouveau period, especially the leaded light windows which were frequently personalised by the purchaser of the new property with their own particular choice of colours and design.

Given below is a mortgage repayment plan attached to the 'A Becket Gardens (Tarring Estate) 1931 Sales brochure' which 21st century readers may find interesting.

Purchasers who do not wish to disturb capital can have a permanent mortgage arranged of about ⅔rds the purchase price, i.e. assuming purchase price is — £1050

Permanent Mortgage would be — — £700

Annual Interest, being the equivalent to rent would be — — — £38 : 10

or 14/9 per week

Cash required — — — £350

If a Purchaser only wishes to pay down a nominal deposit, and would wish to pay off the whole of the purchase amount over say a period of 20 years,

Assuming purchase price is — — £1050

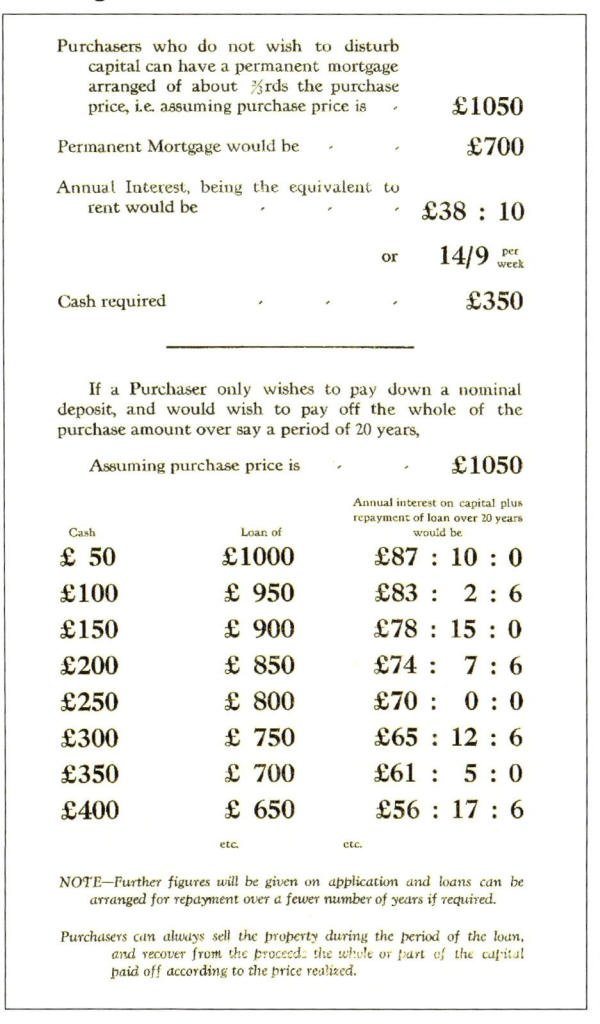

Cash	Loan of	Annual interest on capital plus repayment of loan over 20 years would be
£ 50	£1000	£87 : 10 : 0
£100	£ 950	£83 : 2 : 6
£150	£ 900	£78 : 15 : 0
£200	£ 850	£74 : 7 : 6
£250	£ 800	£70 : 0 : 0
£300	£ 750	£65 : 12 : 6
£350	£ 700	£61 : 5 : 0
£400	£ 650	£56 : 17 : 6
etc.	etc.	

NOTE—Further figures will be given on application and loans can be arranged for repayment over a fewer number of years if required.

Purchasers can always sell the property during the period of the loan, and recover from the proceeds the whole or part of the capital paid off according to the price realized.

Fig. 15 - Mortgage Repayment Plan 1930's.

Chapter 8 - The Architects - Trends in style and rise of 'Art Deco' in 1925

LANCASTER COURT
HURST AVENUE · WEST WORTHING

Fig. 16 - Lancaster Court, Hurst Avenue, Architects: Wood & Kendrick.
16 modern flats, rental of £135 pa.
This brochure also depicts the places of interest in and around Worthing describing the town as 'The Garden Town By The Sea'.

Fig. 17 - Photo Credit: Rob Blarn.
St Thomas a Becket. Architect: Marcus Rainsford Fletcher (1907-1990).

The above photograph was taken two years after a devastating fire in 2018 had swept through all storeys of this shopping centre, as can be seen to the left of the picture. A total of ten flats and five shops were completely destroyed.

Chapter 8 - The Architects - Trends in style and rise of 'Art Deco' in 1925

Fig. 18 - Photo Credit: Rob Blann.
[7]*Onslow Court, Brighton Road; 30 flats and 12 garages.*
Designed by Architect A T W Goldsmith (1892-1972) and built in 1934.

Worthing Architects, Saville Jones has placed this building on their list of local Buildings of Interest and therefore, although not listed to date, gives this iconic building a degree of protection.

Obviously, no expense was spared in the promotion of this ground breaking Art Deco designed property which eulogises all the up-to-date amenities and of course its superb situation overlooking the sea.

Reproduced below are two pages from the original sales brochure.

Fig. 19 -
Onslow Court Brochure Front Cover.

Fig. 20 -
Onslow Court Sales Brochure.

The Houses That George and William Built - Their Life & Times

Chapter 8 - The Architects - Trends in style and rise of 'Art Deco' in 1925

Fig. 21 - Photo Credit: Family Archives.
Art Deco Flats in Clarence Court, Brighton Road, Worthing.
Architect: Marcus Rainsford Fletcher (1907-1990), built in 1936.

Fig. 22 - Photo Credit: Family Archives.
Wellesley Court, Wallace Avenue. Architect: Marcus Rainsford Fletcher (1907-1990).

Fig. 23 -
Photo Credit: Family Archives.
Downview Court, Boundary Road, Worthing.
Architect:
Marcus Rainsford Fletcher
(1907-1990).

Chapter 8 - The Architects - Trends in style and rise of 'Art Deco' in 1925

Fig. 24 - Photo Credit: Family Archives.
Architect: Unknown. Colonnade House, 47 Warwick Street, Worthing. Built 1936.

Fig. 25 - Photo Credit: Family Archives.
Five semi-detached houses, numbers 299-317, Brighton Road with featured green glazed [8]pantile roofs. Architect: [9]Charles Hugh Wallis (1892-1941).

Footnotes

[1] The 'Brutalist' style of architecture came to the fore in the 1950's.
[2] It becomes quite clear on perusing the List of Architects *(pages 109-111)* that there is little evidence of any reputable Architects setting up practice in the Worthing area prior to 1890.
[3] A T W Goldsmith LRIBA and Marcus Rainsford Fletcher had offices at 39 Chapel Road, Worthing in 13 Liverpool Chambers, Worthing.
[4] This idea had already been made in Mrs. Beeton's Book of Household Management in her description of the ideal kitchen layout.
[5] The life of the domestic copper was extended for a few years when mains gas supplies became available and used to heat the water in the copper, no doubt proving more labour saving than the previously used coal and coke.
[6] A little side line to history to say the writer can remember her mother attempting to boil potatoes on the Dining Room fire place during the Blitz of Plymouth in 1941. The house had been built about 1935 so on this occasion particularly, the presence of the mainly unused means of heating was more than appreciated and in fact essential when all else had failed.
[7] Onslow Court was requisitioned during the period of WWII for the use of the French-Canadian Army, as were the houses along the Brighton Road. Additionally, Bill recalls in his memoirs whilst visiting his ailing father in Worthing in either 1941 or 1942 reported, 'One evening, he walked along the road by the sea towards a large block of flats (Onslow Court) he had built about 7 or 8 years earlier. To his astonishment, the road was lined, on the seaward side, with large tanks, nose to tail. Getting an invasion force ready for action, he thought, I wonder how they are going to get them across the English Channel?' Of course, history now tells us that the 'Mulberry Harbours' achieved this apparently almost impossible task, enabling the invasion of Normandy to take place. Authors Note - the date of the Invasion was June 1944.
[8] Pantile tiles are traditionally made of clay and therefore lighter than other roof tile materials such as slate. The tiles were glazed to make them waterproof.
[9] Charles H Wallis (1892-1941) and his wife Olive Wallis lived at 317 Brighton Road. Olive was Godmother to the writer's sister Josephine.

The Houses That George and William Built - Their Life & Times

Chapter 9
George Jonathan Mills (1820-1903) 19th Century Philanthropist

Fig. 26 -
Watercolour painting thought to be of George Jonathan Mills attributed to William Freeman (1784-1877), Norwich School of Painters.

Chapter 9 - George Jonathan Mills (1820-1903) 19th Century Philanthropist

Fig. 27 - Photo Credit: Lorraine, Manchester.
'Colville'[1] 33 Gratwicke Road, Worthing - the residence where George Jonathan Mills lived from 1881 with his second wife Georgiana Riches and their family.

In order to bring this interesting and industrious man into the light, it would be wise to be clear why I have given him the title of '19th Century Philanthropist' at the head of this chapter.

The dictionary defines the word 'philanthropist' as one who does good deeds to others or tries to benefit mankind. I would like to add to this criteria, in as much as I believe the true philanthropist does not make a show of his or her benefactions but ensures that it is carefully either disguised or perhaps carried out through a third party. This being said, there can be no doubt that George Jonathan, who although not publicising his gifts in any way, was very well aware of his own business benefits which might accrue from what appears on the surface to be pure charity.

George Jonathan came from a fairly humble background with his father owning a fruit and vegetable shop in Hastings. However, his young son independently launched himself into business by selling the local fisherman's catch from a small cart pulled by a dog and thereby making his first profit. As time passed, he became a wholesale fish merchant with premises in London's Billingsgate Market. This career proved financially very successful and he was to invest in land in both Lowestoft and Sussex; Worthing in particular, ultimately becoming one of the six richest landowners in the district of Heene *(see Wards Map page 108)*.

Chapter 9 - George Jonathan Mills (1820-1903) 19th Century Philanthropist

It is at this point in this story, that the name George Jonathan Mills starts appearing on the Steere family documents and how his life-changing influence on the writer's grandfather George Edwin Steere came about. Like so many stories there are many strands to this one which binds the whole together, and so perhaps it is best to start with documentary evidence and the basis to this remarkable story.

In the following letter dated 3rd February 1976, received from the author's [2]Aunt Dorothy Steere in which she makes particular mention of George Jonathan Mills and his role in the family.

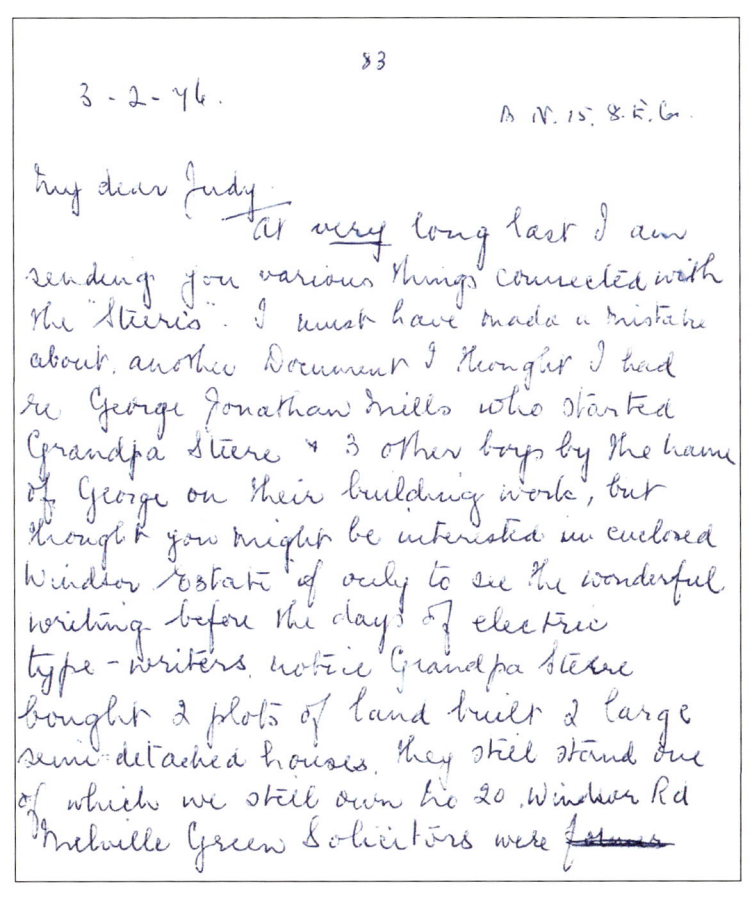

> 83
>
> 3-2-76.
>
> A N. 15. 8. E. 6.
>
> My dear Judy
>
> At very long last I am sending you various things connected with the "Steeres". I must have made a mistake about another Document I thought I had re George Jonathan Mills who started Grandpa Steere & 3 other boys by the name of George on their building work, but thought you might be interested in enclosed Windsor Estate of only to see the wonderful writing before the days of electric type-writers. notice Grandpa Steere bought 2 plots of land built 2 large semi-detached houses. they still stand one of which we still own No 20 Windsor Rd. Melville Green Solicitors were ~~fathers~~

Fig. 28 - Photo Credit: Family Archives.
See Fig. 29 on the following page to see the outer cover of The Windsor Estate Document, referred to in the above letter.

Chapter 9 - George Jonathan Mills (1820-1903) 19th Century Philanthropist

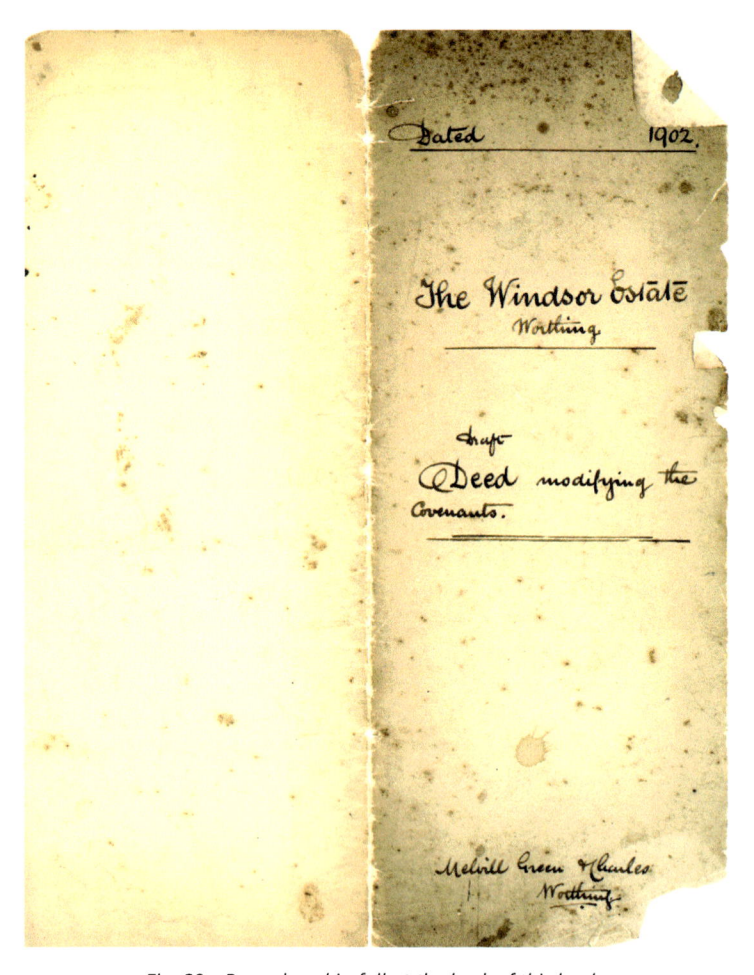

Fig. 29 - Reproduced in full at the back of this book.

This document contains some important information in as much as it mentions two dates, firstly the one on the outside cover which gives 1902 the date on which this Covenant was drawn up and, more significantly, the date 1875 (mentioned on the first page) when the plots of land were first allocated to the named purchasers. It is quite evident that some twenty-seven years had elapsed where no buildings had been erected on any of the plots. This situation whereby valuable building plots had been left unsold and undeveloped for such a long time, gives very strong evidence to George Jonathan's possible thinking that by providing the

Chapter 9 - George Jonathan Mills (1820-1903) 19th Century Philanthropist

four young men named George with a once in a lifetime opportunity to build for themselves on extremely favourable terms, would perhaps kick-start a building boom in this apparently unfavoured part of town.

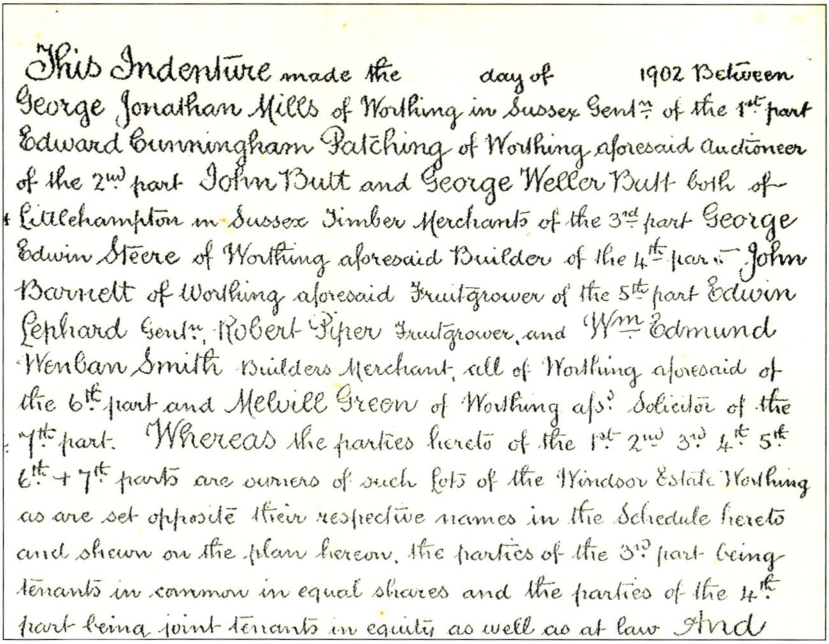

> This Indenture made the   day of   1902 Between George Jonathan Mills of Worthing in Sussex Gent: of the 1st part Edward Cunningham Patching of Worthing aforesaid auctioneer of the 2nd part John Butt and George Weller Butt both of Littlehampton in Sussex Timber Merchants of the 3rd part George Edwin Steere of Worthing aforesaid Builder of the 4th part John Barrett of Worthing aforesaid Fruitgrower of the 5th part Edwin Cephard Gent: Robert Piper Fruitgrower and Wm Edmund Wenban Smith Builders Merchant all of Worthing aforesaid of the 6th part and Melvill Green of Worthing afsd Solicitor of the 7th part. Whereas the parties hereto of the 1st 2nd 3rd 4th 5th 6th + 7th parts are owners of such lots of the Windsor Estate Worthing as are set opposite their respective names in the Schedule hereto and shewn on the plan hereon, the parties of the 3rd part being tenants in common in equal shares and the parties of the 4th part being joint tenants in equity as well as at law And

Fig. 30 -
The Windsor Estate Document (See footnote[3] and Appendix for copy of full document).

Apart from strong family tradition, this letter, and the document referred to, validates the place held by George Jonathan Mills in family history, allied with his important role in not only giving my Grandfather (George Edwin), a helping hand on the ladder to become a fully-fledged builder/developer, but also three other 'boys' referred to in this letter. In terms of accuracy the term 'boy' can be assumed to mean young men, a terminology still in use today.

The verbal family history passed down through the generations, telling us that George Jonathan met George Edwin down at the beach, does not seem implausible as he might well have been walking along the Esplanade and saw a group of boys down on the sea shore, possibly where the Lifeboat was usually launched, and got into conversation with them. Perhaps the young men may have been flattered by the notice of the older man to expand on their own hopes and dreams for the future, or the older man may have gained some private amusement from his conversations with the youths idling among the boats.

The final thought must remain that whatever the place, or time of the meeting/meetings with the four Georges may have been, there can be no doubt that George Jonathan was an excellent judge of character, and by giving such a potentially valuable gift to them, showed a confidence in their integrity and abilities to carry out whatever project they had placed before him.

At this point in the story it is obvious that George Edwin must have both known and kept in touch with the other three boys and therefore any details of their success or failure had been passed down through three generations of the writer's family. Perhaps a note of doubt may creep into this story of the meeting on the beach as it appears 'far-fetched', that four young men should all have the name George, but it should be remembered that there had been four monarchs, between the years 1714 and 1830, of this name so it was not unlikely that the name had gained some popularity with many patriotic parents.

Perhaps to further validate the whole story of the four Georges, one can say that George Jonathan certainly seems to have had a fixation or maybe a special liking for his own name of George. Born in the reign of George IV, he himself certainly had all the appearance of a typical Georgian gentleman of the period. His first little daughter, who sadly died young, was called Georgiana, however, notwithstanding this no doubt painful loss, another daughter was also subsequently named Georgiana when he married his second wife Georgiana Riches.

I stated at the beginning of this chapter that there were many strands to this story and one of these strands, leads to the probability that George Jonathan had already made some sort of prior connection with George Edwin via George's widowed mother. That this connection seems more than likely with the setting up of Charlotte Susan (Blann - George Edwin's mother) in an Art Shop[4] in Worthing, taking her out of the drudgery of her work as a laundress, a fact she stresses in the Census Return of 1881 stating under the 'Rank Profession Occupation' column firmly underlining the words 'formerly a laundress'. It seems that the death of her husband, who was drowned at sea in 1879, may have been the moment when George Jonathan came to the rescue of this family. It cannot be stressed too much that there is definitely some further basis for thinking that there was a connection of some sort with the passing down of George Jonathan's portrait through three generations of the writer's family, and here reproduced at the top of this chapter. Added to this it is also interesting to note that it seems more than possible that the astute businessman, as he always was, had already identified a gap in the market for prints and framing of pictures. It is also quite possible that the idea to set up an Art Shop had occurred to him whilst his portrait was painted, probably no later than 1877, whilst in Lowestoft where he had many business interests.

To return to the story of the four Georges and whatever his motives may have been, quite possibly a combination of his shrewd business mind allied with his undoubted underlying philanthropic aims, the result was he gave each boy a plot of land to develop as they wished but with the caveat that if unused would be returned to their benefactor at the end of a year. How I wish that any document, if such existed, were found laying out the terms of this generous gift or should it be called a 'loan'? If a mid-value estimate of building plots is given of say £100, this in today's values would be approximately £12,000, a not inconsiderable gift.

As far as George Edwin was concerned, he was able to build his first property on his plot and this set him off on his career as a serious developer, but of course this was the first step, but a most important one in reaching this goal. It is not known for certain exactly where this plot was but it seems highly likely it was at one end of the present-day [5]Eastcourt Road, *(see Chapter 10 pages 72-81)* in which Dorothy witnessed her father building in both Eastcourt and Brighton Roads.

Only fragments of information relating to the ultimate outcomes of the histories relating to the three other Georges has been passed down through the generations of the family to this day, some of which are very tenuous indeed. However, in the interests of any researchers of the future I include the few scraps given to the writer by the older members of the family.

The second of the four 'boys' appears likely to have been [6]George Paine (1844-1903) of Broadwater, who in 1887 patented a counterbalance ventilating gear for glass houses, 250,000 of which were in use by 1890. It is not known if the gift of a plot of land (if indeed it did take place) played any part in his experiments and development of his highly successful invention.

A third 'George' sold the turf and purchased ladders enabling him to undertake work for others and presumably fund building on the site; finding the name of this boy will be more difficult. The only, and very brief, tradition relating to the fourth young man says that he was not able to conclude his agreement with George Jonathan and the land was returned after the twelve months were up. It should be said that this latter part of the fate of the fourth George is based on a very small thread of information and the exact circumstances are not known. Despite this, it is pertinent to the fact that the gift/loan of the land would not be the end of the project and all would have found it difficult to find the finances to purchase building materials and maybe employ builders to carry out the work and this may have been the stumbling block that resulted in this case of an incomplete agreement. At this point however George Edwin Steere has many advantages in his favour. Firstly, he was himself a Master Builder and would not have been reliant on other skilled workmen to carry out the work for him. He also had worked for many years with a local builder who may have been willing to supply him with materials to carry out the first project with may be an agreement to share in the ensuing profits when the property was sold.

The writer has lived most of her life with the water colour portrait of a Georgian gentleman hanging on the wall without knowing who he was and if there was any connection with the family. Curiosity eventually made the removal of the back cover essential in the hope that a name would be written inside. However, written in pencil across the back is

Chapter 9 - George Jonathan Mills (1820-1903) 19th Century Philanthropist

'Who is this man?' Now after two years research and the most fortunate gift by my aunt of the Deed reproduced here *(see page 67 Fig. 30)* I am sure I now know. The only regret, I wish I had known him.

The final words should be left to those inscribed on his [7]gravestone at Heene Cemetery - "Whatsoever thy hand findeth to do, do it with thy might!" Eccles 9,10. A worthy quotation which in my opinion encapsulates the man.

George Jonathan Mills is buried together with his wife Georgiana at Heene Cemetery, Worthing, Sussex. He left an Estate of 15.8 million pounds in 2020 values.

Footnotes

[1]Carlton Colville is a district of Lowestoft in Norfolk where Georgiana Riches had lived prior to marriage.

[2]Dorothy May Steere (1901-1988) on the death of her husband George Edwin Steere in 1969 took over the management of the family properties and was therefore in a position to have complete access to all the documents relating to her late father-in-law George Edwin Steere.

[3]Edwin Lephard, (one of the names featured in the Windsor document) owner of threshing and traction engine company in a business Lephard & Paine. This connection between the Paine and Lephard families, certainly in this case in relation to business activities, does perhaps lead to some prior connection between the two men via G.J. Mills and his 'gift' of land to George Paine (one of the four Georges). Furthermore, Edwin Lephard was also another Worthing property owner and together with George Jonathan Mills developed the area of Heene. George Jonathan Mills is listed amongst the six main Heene landowners which included the Duke of Norfolk.

[4]It appears that the Art Shop sold prints and pictures and possibly provided a picture framing service carried out by the then youthful George Edwin as recorded in Dorothy's Memoirs.

[5]2 Eastcourt Road, built by George Edwin became the family home where my mother Dorothy grew up.

[6]I am indebted to Rosemary Pearson and the Friends of Broadwater for information regarding George Paine and his family.

[7]Grave No. NES Row: 6, Plot 17; Georgiana died in 1913 (born 1848).

The Houses That George and William Built - Their Life & Times

Chapter 10
George Edwin Steere (1863-1926)

Fig. 31 - Photo Credit: Otto Brown, Worthing.
George Edwin Steere.

Family background

George Edwin Steere was born on 16th September 1863 to George Carter Steere and his wife Charlotte Susan Blann, whilst living at 27 New Town, Worthing.

The row of stucco terrace cottages, including number 27, no longer exist having been demolished in 1959. This was a very poor area indeed in which to bring up their family of six, with an unsavoury reputation as the base for unruly elements, such as the anti-Salvation Army and anti-police mobs.

However, [1]George Carter Steere, a fisherman with a wife who on the 1881 Census is listed as 'formerly a Laundress', apparently managed to place their two sons in positions where they could be trained as carpenter/joiners, ensuring their contribution to the family income at an early age.

As can be seen from Dorothy's Memoirs, George had been well trained in all areas of house-building during his time of employment by Mr Blaker, and in fact at the commencement of his own business, he could be termed a Master Builder. At this time George would have been helped by the availability of several [2]Pattern Books which he would have been able to purchase. Therefore, it is quite probable that most, if not all of the houses he was to build, would be based on these.

It is a fallacy that Architects would be required in any building development at this period and probably, if needed, a Surveyor would be called in as required on a particular development, perhaps in the early planning relating to the layout. By 1887, developers were required to submit their plans to the local authority and should this not be obtained before building commenced, then this building could be pulled down - a serious loss to the builder.

My Aunt Dorothy Steere, wife of George Edwin junior, told me in a letter written in 1976 that Grandpa Steere 'was a nice jolly man and retired when he was 35, although I say it, he was very fond of me, and the first time I went to tea he told George he liked me, and he was to bring me again!'

George's son-in-law Bill described him in his later years as 'a very big man with a red face, green-blue eyes, almost turquoise, white hair and a moustache' and added 'he would have passed as a prosperous Spanish gentleman of about 65 with a liking for the good things of life, especially eating and drinking.' Bill became very fond of the old man and no doubt they would have had many subjects in common to talk about and perhaps the older man would have given some useful advice along the way.

There is no doubt that George was a well-known and liked character in Worthing with the local baker baking his favourite white Viennese loaf and the actress Margaret Brennan (one of George's tenants) making him the Executor of her Will. In this Will she left a personal gift to his wife Emily of a box of beautiful kid gloves, pale lavender, soft pink and pearl grey amongst other delicate colours. The annual gift to George's little daughter Dorothy of a child's [3]model hat, sent from the well-known London store Peter Robinsons, was a further mark of her esteem *(see page 25 Fig. 3)*.

"In the first years of our [4]parents' marriage, they were not very well off. They did well enough but father had not really been able to get started to build more than one house at a time. More land was eventually bought and he could then start to become a developer and build whole streets. Firstly, two or three houses in Northcourt Road, then the whole of [5]Eastcourt Road and, then, one side of Westcourt Road. Six or so in Bridge Road, a small terrace in Southcourt Road and some shops in Tarring Road and two large houses in Heene Road.' 'In the summer months of the years my father was building the 'Marina', the houses which we still possess, and which provide some income, he would take me with him, and after viewing the men's work and progress on the buildings, we would cross the road to the beach."

Other areas/buildings which can be credited to George Edwin, is a large part south of Broadwater, the Anchorage Hotel, Shoreham, The Ingleside Hotel and The Wolsey, both in Brighton Road, together with all of Windsor Road and Navarino Road.

John Nathaniel Brice (1828-1887), the writer's great grandfather and

Emily's father, had, while still living in London, made some unwise investments in the [6]Heene Estate Company. The name of this company can still be seen on old legal documents, also mentioned in A M Rowland and T P Hudson's book 'A History of Worthing'. When the company went bankrupt, John Nathaniel had a choice of losing his money or taking possession of the land in Worthing, he chose the latter.

The Brice family house in Worthing was named [7]'Field Lodge' situated in [8]Teville Road and at the bottom of the garden ran the Teville stream (now taken underground to Lancing where it forms the Broadlands Leisure Lake). The Teville Road house has long gone with houses and busy tarmac roads with traffic lights taking its place.

It is important at this stage to expand on the known background to John Nathaniel's life as it has a bearing not only on the Heene Estate but also the possible prior connection with another important person entering George Edwin's life, namely George Jonathan Mills.

John Nathaniel Brice was a Thames River Pilot who also owned a [9]Ships Chandlers shop in, I believe Holborn, London, where all of his ten children (eight sons and two daughters, the eldest of who was Emily the author's grandmother), were born. He had a key to Gray's Inn Gardens where the children were allowed to play, which implies that the family home was situated close by.

It is fortunate that we know how John Nathaniel looked, as the writer has had passed down to her, a large double-sided brooch containing a hand-tinted photograph of John Nathaniel and on the reverse side is portrayed his wife and young son *(see Fig. Nos. 32a & 32b on page 77)*.

We do also have some idea of the character of the man as his descendants have passed down a picture of a deeply religious man strictly adhering to observance of Sunday as a day when the children's toys were locked away and his wife enduring the reading to her from Sturgeon's book of sermons.

Without doubt, John Nathaniel was a respected person in the business community as evidenced by the Award of the Freedom of the City of London in 1849 *(see page 77 Fig. 33)*.

It may have been the conjunction of more than one event in John Nathaniel's life that made the move to Worthing inevitable. Sometime in the late 1880's he may have been experiencing the first symptoms of consumption and with the collapse of the Heene Estate Company, in which he was the major shareholder, led to the family's move to a more salubrious climate.

It seems in hindsight, that the development of the land in Heene by John Nathaniel, was the foundation of the family's modest fortunes and with the eldest of his two daughters, Emily, having married George Edwin Steere in 1889, it is entirely possible that some settlement or marriage portion enabled George to accelerate his start in adult life. However, fortune had stepped in at an earlier stage, as can be seen in Chapter 9, with his meeting with the philanthropist George Jonathan Mills. The [10]exact date or place of this meeting is not known, but it seems that it either occurred just prior to, or at the end of, the 1880's, after his father's death in 1879.

In order to bring some clarity to the areas in which George Jonathan Mills and John Nathaniel Brice may have met and even conducted business with each other, in the period 1860-1880, whilst they were both resident in London, the following points need to be taken into consideration. Foremost, was their mutual interest in the fishing industry, with John Nathaniel owning a Ships Chandlers shop and George Jonathan listed as a Fish Wholesalesman. Both men were awarded the Freedom of the City of London, with George Jonathan Mills based at offices in [11]Billingsgate where John Nathaniel owned some of the ground rents. In later years both men retired to Worthing, and perhaps their mutual interests continued with the development of land in the 1880's, especially land at Heene. Despite all these tenuous connections, several quite substantial, no absolute proof of either business, social or family connections can be found to date. It is important to establish whether the gift of land to George Edwin had originated through these possible friendly/business connections between the two men.

Chapter 10 - George Edwin Steere (1863-1926)

Fig. 32a

Fig. 32b

Photo Credits: Family Archives.
32a - John Nathaniel Brice, Thames River Pilot and Ships Chandler.
32b - Emily Brice (Peirce) with son John (Jack) Nathaniel.

Fig. 33 -
John Nathaniel Brice's Copy of the Document - Freedom of the City of London, dated 1849. A complete and enlarged copy of this document can be found in Appendix item 10 (page 116).

By the time of the 1901 Census, George Edwin who was then 37, was described as a builder and employer. So, the family tradition that he 'retired' at 35 could only refer to his finally leaving paid work as an employee of the local builder, [12]Blaker.

"While father was building Eastcourt Road, there was a temporary carpenter's shop or working place, with hastily erected timber walls and a corrugated iron roof, this was almost where numbers 21 and 23 Eastcourt now stand. This was moved as work progressed up the road for the permanent carpenter's shop, near the railway lines and put into use later."

The Houses That George and William Built - Their Life & Times   77

This Carpenter's shop was built close to George Edwin's house in Eastcourt Road and the young Dorothy loved to visit this busy workshop, enjoying the clean smell of the newly sawn wood and to pick up the curls of shaved wood lying under the benches. The men would make little wooden toys out of off cuts to amuse the little visitor.

It was probably in this permanent workshop that George's two sons, George junior and his younger brother, Freddie kept their rabbits. I regret to say that the intention was that they should be ultimately destined for the pot but when the day came their mother rebelled and said the rabbits should be set free, adding that she hated to see animals kept in cages. So, probably not too unwillingly, the two boys took the pet rabbits up to Chanctonbury Ring where they were released. Dorothy tells in her Memoirs that over the years she had heard of reports of black rabbits having been seen in the area and one can only assume that some of the does survived to breed with the local wild rabbits. I wonder if their descendants survive to this day?

This was not the only other extra-curricular activity taking place in the workshop, which situated as it was, so close to the two boys' home, should see them persuade the carpenters to make them a sledge and also embark on two large kites which would give them and their little sister Dorothy great pleasure. It seems that their father George either turned a blind eye to all this extra work taking his men away from their normal tasks, or perhaps he actively encouraged his son's activities, I would like to think so.

Although George Edwin's good nature was perhaps taken advantage of, being easily persuaded to buy that extra round of drinks at the pub (good old George, such a sport!), he did indeed have another side to his character which is shown by the fact that finding one of his friends in serious financial trouble, he sold one of his own houses to provide the funds to rescue him. As can be imagined this caused some alarm amongst his family, particularly his wife who found out the cause of the 'missing' house from the list of properties at the Estate Office. To put a different light on the affair, this may have been George Edwin's way of repaying the similar benefit he had received at the hands of George Jonathan Mills ten or twenty years earlier. However, cynics may perhaps say he was duped by his so-called friend. We will never know, but I would like to think that it was a one-time humanitarian act given to a friend in need.

During these early years as a developer, George's friends would laugh at his building in the Brighton Road area, so far out of town as they perceived it, but today these elegant houses built across the road from the beach and sea, offer uninterrupted coastal views from their attractive little balconies and front rooms, remaining today as sought-after residential properties.

Each of these Brighton Road terrace houses had between four and five bedrooms, with the largest room fronting the seaward side of the house. 'Wolsey', 'Olinda' and 'Marina' were all names used early on for some of these properties built by George Edwin, names still remaining today. Dorothy tells us in her Memoirs that as a little girl she witnessed the 'Marina' as it was being built. It is very probable that the 'Baltimore' was named by George Edwin as a reference to his two sons who were living and working as Architects in America at that time.

Fig. 34 - Photo Credit: Catherine Gwynne. The Baltimore Guest House, Brighton Road, Worthing in 2018. One of a row of sixteen terrace houses built by George Edwin in the Brighton Road.

George Edwin lived to meet his daughter's young husband 'Bill', who is also the subject of this book, and his part in the story of Worthing unfolds in Chapter 11. George Edwin Steere is buried at the Broadwater Cemetery, Worthing, Sussex.

Chapter 10 - George Edwin Steere (1863-1926)

Fig. 35 - Photo Credit: by kind permission of the owner.
The Windsor Hotel, [13]Windsor Road, Worthing, built by George Edwin.
(The hotel was originally built as four houses).

Footnotes

[1]George Carter Steere is commemorated with other men of the Worthing Lifeboat crews in the RNLI Memorial Garden situated at Splash Point on Worthing seafront.

[2]Pattern books such as the comprehensive and detailed book published in 1839 by the Architect Dr. John Claudius Loudon (1783-1843) entitled 'An Encyclopaedia of Cottage, Farm, and Villa Architecture and Furniture' with over 50 Architects etc, contributing to this monumental work.

[3]The writer was given by her mother some of the pale pink roses made of soft velvet and silk which had originally adorned one of these hats.

[4]George Edwin Steere's marriage to Emily Grace Brice took place in 1889 *(see Family Tree on page 102).*

[5]George Edwin Steere's family lived in 2 Eastcourt Road, an end house that he had built.

[6]In 1863, William Westbrooke Richardson, who owned most of the manor of Heene, sold his land to the Heene Estate Land Company, which in turn sold the southern part of its land to the West Worthing Investment Company in 1864. In 1865, the property of the two companies became the new town of West

Worthing, which was intended to be an upmarket resort and residential area in its own right. In 1873, West Worthing was extended westwards up to the boundary with the parish of Goring at George V Avenue. The term West Worthing is still in use today *(see Map on page 105)*.

[7] Perhaps the name 'Field Lodge' was inspired by happy earlier days when the family walked in Holborn's Gray's Inn Gardens, possibly entering through the 'Field Court' gate.

[8] This information regarding The Teville Stream is taken from D Robert Elleray's Millennium Encyclopaedia of Worthing History.

[9] Ships Chandlers; a place where basic supplies such as canvas and cordage were sold by a retailer.

[10] The first meeting with George Jonathan Mills is mentioned in Chapter 9.

[11] In fact shares in the ground rents of Billingsgate Market were passed down through the generations when Dorothy was left some of these shares in his Will by her Uncle Jack Brice (1853-1928).

[12] George Edwin was on very cordial terms with his ex-employer as Dorothy reports – "During the 'fever year' the small family were free from this infection for father actually carried buckets of water from the pure well of the Blaker's house. No tap water was used to drink but only for washing."

[13] See Chapter 9 *(page 63)* where the Windsor Estate document relates to the land at Windsor Road.

The Houses That George and William Built - Their Life & Times

Chapter 11
Leslie William Waterman (1903-1990)

*Fig. 36 - Photo Credit: Walter Gardiner, Worthing.
Leslie William Waterman.*

Family background

Bill's father, Edward Charles Waterman (1864-1945), had moved to Worthing from Bishops Stortford in Hertfordshire, where he had sold his business. Now in 1920, the date it is estimated when he made this move, he was 56 and wished to retire to a town where his wife had close relatives and would provide the warmer climate more suited to recovering invalids. Both his wife and youngest son had been victims of the devastating Spanish 'flu' which had swept the country just after the 1914-18 War.

On taking up residence in Worthing, the still active man served on the Urban District Council and also on the Borough Council following this later by being elected Chairman of the local Conservative Party. He was also a faithful member of his local Church and an enthusiastic Worthing Choir member.

Edward Charles, having established himself in many areas of both the business and the social life of Worthing, was more than suited to help his young son take his own first steps to become a property developer. However, perhaps unexpectedly, it was the younger man who was able to point his father the way to substantially improve his own financial position by investing in property development. Subsequently, with much improved income, Edward Charles was able to purchase a well-built semi-detached house overlooking the Channel for his disabled son Earnest, who had by now a wife and four children to support on a tiny pension and also build a substantial bungalow on the Littlehampton Road close to the Thomas a Becket junction for himself. This was an important development in the family's life, particularly that of Bill who had always felt that he had not done enough to help his brother and so through helping his father to a more comfortable and secure retirement, he had at the same time, by extension, been able to help his ailing brother.

Fig. 37 - Photo Credit: Walter Gardiner.
Edward Charles Waterman shaking hands with the Duke Of York (later King George VI) in Worthing on his visit 30th May 1928.

Leslie William Waterman Early Days:
The following article written by my sister, Josephine Jones[1] gives an insight into Bill's early formative years

"My Father 'Bill' as he was known in his more mature years was a tall, thin, lanky youth when the 1914/18 War broke out. His much older brother 'Ernest' had gone off to fight in the trenches whilst his younger brother was still at school.

Bill's happiest days were to go off for a day's fishing with a 1lb bag of broken biscuits costing one penny. He could 'tickle' trout with his hand, and was fast enough to put his long legs to good use by running down a rabbit and catch it by its ears. All he wanted to do was to be in the country and eventually become a farmer.

All the boyish country pursuits stopped when he was sent by his parents to a farm where he was employed in the breaking in of young cart horses which were needed in increasing numbers to pull the heavy guns in France. No doubt his parents thought he would be safe there and as the boy was so keen to make farming his career it seemed a sensible choice in the circumstances. I remember my father telling me how life was tough and one of his main roles was the care of the unbroken colts. 'I soon learnt to jump the 6 foot partitions between the stalls from a standing position to escape the very large and potentially lethal hooves of the untrained colts.'

The hours were very long and the farmer worked the boys very hard, no doubt glad to have this cheap labour. In fact, I later understood that my grandparents had paid the farmer a fee but whether this was for his bed and board or to teach him the rudiments of farming life I do not know. I am personally of the opinion the reasoning behind this arrangement was perhaps to steer their son away from this particular career as he was academically clever and they thought to cure him of this desire to be a farmer. Unfortunately, as it turned out this was probably one of the worst decisions they were to make for him which nearly became fatal.

It appears that the farmer's wife had great difficulty in feeding these *young lads doing a man's job and 'Bill' said the endless diet of rabbit (no doubt plentiful on the farm) impelled the boys to get together and do a bit of pheasant poaching on neighbouring land. I am glad to say none of them were caught by the Game Keeper as punishment could have been severe. Maybe he turned a 'blind eye' on these rare escapades by the boys. I would like to think so. In later life Father was ashamed to admit to this event in trying to find a supplement to their unvaried and insufficient diet.*

The work finally ended when my father collapsed from ²exhaustion and had to return home. He was so ill that the Doctor told his parents he did not expect him to recover, but 'Bill's' determination to live brought him through, but he never returned to work on the farm again. Despite all of this my Father retained his love of farming and his life-long interest in horses.

Bill's brother did survive the horrors of France, but returned with Trench fever and died a few years later as a result."

It is good to pause in this narrative of Bill's life to see how the events of the past few years had affected his outlook. Undoubtedly, he was most affected by the return of his soldier brother, a broken man with the long-lasting effects of ³Trench Fever from which he never recovered. Despite the difference of twelve years between the two brothers, the comparatively young and strong Bill felt an increasing sense of responsibility for his older brother.

There is another element in his character, and an important one, that should perhaps be taken into consideration, and this was that Bill had a social conscience which impelled him to seek a way to provide returning servicemen the means of earning a wage when work was not available in this post World War I era. The knowledge that thousands of returning soldiers were without work, his own brother included, may very well all be factors in his thinking at this period.

Father also had a strong, in-built work ethic, and was thorough and meticulous in all his work, whether cleaning out a stable, constructing an important document or just a routine confirmatory letter - all received his total concentration and care. It was this close attention to detail, allied with his understanding of the property market, no doubt gained when he later worked in the Estate Agents in Worthing, that allowed him to seize opportunities whenever they arose.

Bill later described himself as being ahead of his times as he introduced his builder partners to the concept of bulk buying. He left them aghast when he purchased the entire production of facing bricks from one yard and a million common bricks from another, but as he said he was buying wholesale to sell retail i.e the houses. Also on this theme, his land purchases were by the acre and not a plot or few plots at a time, thereby maximising his profit margins. Once his partners could see the building costs substantially reduced in every direction, they soon took on board this new way of land development, happy to leave this part of the business in this young man's very capable hands. It should be said that Bill never took any Managing Director's salary or expenses for his work as this was not part of his initial aim.

As in the case of George Edwin, fate intervened when, on visiting the hairdresser, he found a local newspaper left behind by a customer and idly scanning its pages, saw an advertisement where a position as a Junior Clerk at a local Estate Agents was offering £2 per week with two weeks holiday pay and all the other usual holidays. This was riches indeed compared to his five shillings per week pocket money given to him at the farm for a seventy-hour working week involving heavy manual labour. Despite the misgivings of his parents, he decided to apply and to his surprise got the job which turned out to be in effect the clerk on the Reception Desk. However, when applying for the job he had absolutely no idea of the size and scale of his new employers who not only had the Estate Agents where he worked but also owned large Auction Rooms which were attached to the office where Bill was working.

The times at the desk could be very quiet with little or nothing to do for hours on end and, to keep himself occupied, he started to delve into the Property Register which was on his desk and realising that he knew nothing of his new environment, he began to study the details of every house, shop, piece of land or other property listed in it. This led him to a town map, which in turn sent him cycling around every street and road mentioned in the Register. This was helped by one of his tasks which was to collect the weekly rents from various cottages and the quarterly rents of several houses managed by the Estate Office.

Also looking for progress in his new employment, he attended evening lectures at night school at a local [4]Technical College. The course included Land Surveying, building materials and their uses and prices, the law of contract of Landlord and Tenant, Drainage and Sanitation, Valuation and Valuation Tables, Ordinance sheets and their uses, Estate Management and various other aspects of property affairs.

It was only by catching the last suitable train to attend his lectures in Brighton after work, that he was able to continue with the full course, returning home by 10.30 in the evening. All his weekends were taken up with homework ready for the next week's sessions. To add to his already packed schedule, the Estate Office remained open until 10pm on Saturdays, so it was only Bill's determination that he would work towards a better situation in life which carried him through what was a very tight and demanding schedule. Happily, all the work he put into this new career paid off and to his surprise he was able to pass the Auctioneers Institute Examinations without any great difficulty.

As time passed, he struck up a friendship with one of his colleagues who had a desk next to his in the office, and the two young men found they worked very well as a team finally finding themselves with a golden opportunity to buy a plot of land on very easy terms, but where would they find the necessary £50 deposit? After talking to their families, to their surprise, their two Mothers said they would loan the money and this was their first venture into land and property development. The nascent [5]partnership flourished and it was at this time that the plot situated in an old Apple Orchard in a first-class position on the outskirts of the town, just north of Tarring Village, came up for sale and Bill decided to keep this himself to build on at a later date. This bungalow was eventually to be named [6]'Apple Tree Cottage', pictured on the next page.

Chapter 11 - Leslie William Waterman (1903-1990)

It was also at this period that Bill met the young woman who would be his future wife, Dorothy Steere *(see Family Tree page 102)*. Dorothy was on a visit with her parents in Worthing where she was recuperating from a [7]serious ear operation.

Bill had first met Dorothy at a friend's house just a few days prior to his visit on business to the property developer and builder George Edwin Steere, and on being asked to escort Dorothy home from a party, he was astonished to find himself on the same doorstep he had visited only a few days before.

Fig. 38 - Photo Credit: Walter Gardiner, Worthing. Dorothy wearing the 1930's fashionable amber bead necklace.

Fig. 39 - Photo Credit: Family Archives. Apple Tree Cottage, Rectory Road, Worthing.

In time, Bill became very fond of the old man, Dorothy's father, now retired, and no doubt he was able to pass on useful information to the younger man who was so eager to learn. In fact, Bill sat up all night with the then dying man to give the family some respite at this distressing time.

Chapter 11 - Leslie William Waterman (1903-1990)

*Fig. 40 - Photo Credit: Family Archives.
Apple Tree Cottage Sitting Room with door open to the garden.*

Dorothy and Bill were married in 1925 and Apple Tree Cottage built by Bill in 1926, was their first married home. Dorothy recalls that the cottage cost them £500 to build.

*Fig. 41 - Photo Credit: Family Archives.
Apple Tree Cottage Bedroom.*

Note the Art Noveau decorations, tapestry behind the bed and central 'lantern' shape lampshade. The furniture and fittings of Apple Tree Cottage reflected the then fashionable and far-reaching Arts and Crafts Movement and items such as the hand-made wooden door latches were a feature.

Fig. 42 - Photo Credit: Family Archives.
[8]*Frank and Ada Matley in the garden at Chantry Cottage, 1929 - the first owners of this neighbouring property also built by Bill.*

Before this purchase of Bill's and Dorothy's future home, the two young men had a second venture which really set them up as property speculators and developers, putting them in a position to secure banking facilities and employ architects and builders to carry out their numerous schemes. This opportunity involved land on a hillside overlooking the town which from their point of view had every advantage that a building site could have. They were on a southern slope, dry, well drained, with wide views over land and sea, and all the main services were available. This land was at that time cultivated as a [9]Lavender farm by a local Nurseryman, but he was willing to sell only on the proviso that he took his crop before the sale was completed. This situation was not surprising in itself, when on another occasion the plot that Bill purchased was left by the departing vendor with a large crop of unharvested blackcurrant bushes. The frugal couple, Dorothy and Bill, unwilling to let such a delicious crop go to waste, spent their evenings picking all the fruit from the bushes before the builders could start their work. No doubt Dorothy used all her skills in making jam and bottling the valuable fruit. It should be remembered that 'Blackcurrant Tea' was given to invalids and children when sick, and as we now know this was indeed a source of Vitamin 'C' before the tablets etc., now available from the Chemist's shop. Of course, when taking up residence at 'Apple Tree Cottage' they would also be supplied with plentiful fruit in season. The original owner of the plot retained land behind the cottage and continued with his market gardening activities.

The activities of the partners did not pass unnoticed by the firm who had benefited from the extra business the two young men had brought and Bill's weekly wages doubled to £4 per week which, in light of the money he and his partner were generating in their spare time, was laughable in view of their present earnings in land development.

Over time the two young men parted with Bill's partner inheriting another business and it therefore became time for him to launch out on his own. The opportunities were plentiful but to embark on large and expensive building schemes may have seemed, in hindsight, to have been both risky and financially hazardous with the recent Wall Street Crash of 1929 and the years of Depression in the 1930's. In this financial climate it either took bravery or a large amount of self-belief to embark on large building schemes undertaken by Bill's newly formed partnership with first one and then a second builder.

Many Architects, including George Edwin's two sons would adhere to the ethos of handmade rather than machine made furniture and fittings when they built their own semi-detached bungalows in King's Road, Lancing in the late 1920's. My sister and I found these cottages rather like houses where the three bears might have lived, quaint and rather fun!

George Edwin had an advantage over his future son in law in as much as he did not have to directly ally himself with a specific builder or building firm as he was in effect his own builder employing the men he required for each build. Bill, on the other hand, if he wished to carry out his building plans, needed a builder he could trust and therefore took as a partner George Victor Jeffery, establishing the firm, 'Jeffery & Co', later taking on a further partner who was also a builder as the business rapidly expanded when the firm was registered as 'Jeffery Houses.'

By 1936, a very confident and highly successful Bill employed Mowlems to construct a show flat at Olympia to which he took his two little daughters who found the 'pretend' grass the most memorable part of their visit!

The two following photographs are of 66 Goring Road, Worthing (formerly Barclays Bank). Architect: Marcus Rainsford Fletcher (1907-1990) built in 1936.

Fig. 43 - Photo Credit: Family Archives.
1936 - Note the original Art Deco roof line not present in the 2020 photograph below.

Fig. 44 - Photo Credit: L Manchester.
66 Goring Road in 2020.

Bill was to say that this development on Goring Road was his most ambitious project and the one he was most proud. In fact, the Architect's original drawing of the Bank hung above his desk for most of his life.

It was not until a post second World War visit to Worthing when, still a teenager, I was surprised to see the Station Master come out to greet my father and say "We will not have to delay the trains for you today, Mr. Waterman!" Looking for an explanation, I learnt that this had exactly been the situation in those pre-war years. As the employer of hundreds of local men that in fact the trains were delayed for him in his pursuit of further business, for not only his own firm, but the town's considerable workforce. It has to be said that throughout his life his inability to arrive on time was well known and despite this at times annoying fault, his charm and upon arrival his complete dedication to the work in hand giving more than 100% to any task made most forgive this foible.

The fact that Bill was remembered approximately ten years after he left Worthing is a fitting tribute to the lasting beneficial effect he had had on the town. This can be seen from the two articles written by Rob Blann in the January and February 1995 issues of the West Sussex Gazette and reproduced at the back of this book, including pictures of both Clarence Court and St Thomas a Becket whilst under construction. Unfortunately, better quality photographs were unobtainable.

Bill and his family went through hard times both financially and in terms of health, but they all survived the war and with it a return to Bill's early and most successful career in property management. By the late 1950's he was operating from offices in Westminster as an International Development Consultant, so how Bill fared in the years between would certainly make another book about this clever, fascinating and it should be said, at times, difficult character genuinely valued and appreciated by his many friends, most especially by his own family.

Bill's ashes are buried in his parents' grave at Durrington Cemetery, Worthing, Sussex.

Footnotes

[1] This article can be seen on "Yourmemories.co.uk" website.

[2] My sister Josephine, the writer of this piece on Bill's early years was incorrect he had collapsed from the results of catching Spanish 'Flu'.

[3] Trench Fever refers to the infection caused by a body louse, particularly prevalent in the soldiers serving in the Trenches of the 1914/18 War. Most would recover from this infection but a small percentage did not, as in the case of Ernest.

[4] This would become the Brighton College of Technology.

[5] Bill would have been in his early twenties at this stage in his career.

[6] 'Apple Tree Cottage' has been re-named today as 'Apple Trees', although sadly, all the trees have now gone.

[7] This operation is mentioned in Chapter 6, footnote 7.

[8] According to the information given by Ada Matley to her Goddaughter (the writer) Frank Matley (1866-1947) had been asked by the then Duke of York to set up Boys Camps in New Zealand. This information to date has yet to be verified but there was certainly a very impressive 'Bill' as it was known of the sword fish hung across the lintel of their sun room, a fascinating object to be admired and wondered at by a little girl!

[9] Lavender was grown on a commercial basis providing essential oils for the manufacture of Eau de Cologne, scented soaps etc. This herb was also burned aromatically in rooms of invalids.

APPENDIX

Item No.

1. The Windsor Estate, Worthing Draft Deed modifying the Covenant 1902 *(pages 96-101).*

2. Family Tree *(page 102).*

3. List of Buildings (1936) designed by known Architects *(page 103).*

4. Population and Houses Graph *(page 104).*

5. Maps *(pages 105-108).*

6. Architects & Eras *(pages 109-111).*

7. Significant Dates *(page 112).*

8. Rob Blann Newspaper Articles *(pages 113-114).*

9. Before Clarence Court *(page 115).*

10. Freedom of the City of London Document *(page 116).*

Appendix - item 1 - The Windsor Estate

The Windsor Estate, Worthing (1)

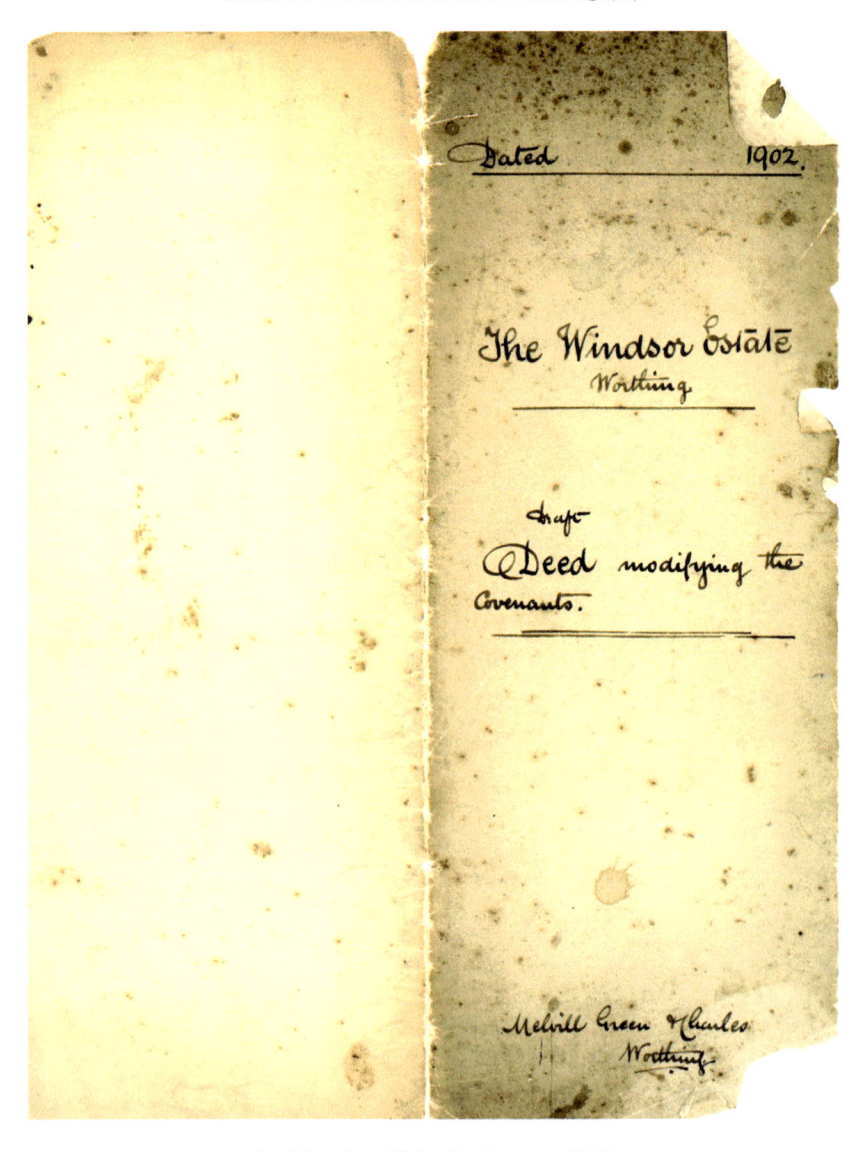

Dated 1902

The Windsor Estate
Worthing

Draft
Deed modifying the
Covenants.

Melvill Green & Charles
Worthing

Draft Deed modifying the Covenant 1902.

The Windsor Estate, Worthing (2)

This Indenture made the   day of   1902 Between George Jonathan Mills of Worthing in Sussex Gent. of the 1st part Edward Cunningham Patching of Worthing aforesaid Auctioneer of the 2nd part John Butt and George Weller Butt both of Littlehampton in Sussex Timber Merchants of the 3rd part George Edwin Steere of Worthing aforesaid Builder of the 4th part. John Barnett of Worthing aforesaid Fruitgrower of the 5th part Edwin Sephard Gent., Robert Piper Fruitgrower, and Wm Edmund Wenban Smith Builders Merchant, all of Worthing aforesaid of the 6th part and Melvill Green of Worthing afs. Solicitor of the 7th part. Whereas the parties hereto of the 1st 2nd 3rd 4th 5th 6th & 7th parts are owners of such lots of the Windsor Estate Worthing as are set opposite their respective names in the Schedule hereto and shown on the plan hereon, the parties of the 3rd part being tenants in common in equal shares and the parties of the 4th part being joint tenants in equity as well as at law And whereas the said lots are bound by covenants contained in Conveyances to them, or to their predecessors in title in 1875 or implied from the said land being part of a building scheme to the effect following namely:-

First. That the owner will not erect or set up or permit or suffer to be erected or set up upon his lot any building erection or projection whatsoever in front of the building lines namely within 35 feet of Windsor Road, 30 feet of Brighton Road and 25 feet of Church Walk save only and except fence walls not exceeding 4 feet in height from the ground of dead work and not exceeding 9 ft in height at the most including rails (if any) and every other part thereof.

Margin notes: If any owner has in any way altered his interest by settlement mortgage or the like the assent of all persons interested should be obtained. M.G. & G.

Draft Deed modifying the Covenant 1902 (continued).

The Windsor Estate, Worthing (3)

2ndly. That the owner will not erect or set up or permit or suffer to be erected or set up upon his lot any building or erection whatsoever other than detached or semi-detached dwellinghouses and proper coach houses stabling outhouses & other offices suitable to be used with such dwelling houses save only houses facing the Brighton Road which may form a row or terrace.

3rdly That the owner will not at any time erect or build or permit to be erected or built any dwellinghouse which shall be of less value than £600 exclusive of the site and outbuildings, except a pair of semi detached dwellinghouses of the full value of £1000 for the pair exclusive of the site and outbuildings.

4thly That the owner will not carry on or permit or suffer to be carried on on his lot any trade business or calling whatsoever or anything of the nature thereof but will use the same and all erections to be thereon as and for private residences only save only and except the professions of a Dentist Accoucheur Surgeon or Physician (but not so as to permit the reception for reward of any lunatic patient or person of unsound mind) Attorney or Solicitor or Keeper of a School for the children of the gentry & nobility and so as there be no sign of or thing used exclusively or principally in any such profession visible from the front of any house other than at the most a small and gentlemanlike inscription of the name & profession of the person or persons there exercising any such profession and in case of the said medical professions a neat coloured glass lamp without inscription thereon.

5thly Will not suffer any clothes to be hung out where the same may be visible from the road nor suffer any bricks or weeds to be burnt on any part of the said hereditaments respectively

Draft Deed modifying the Covenant 1902 (continued).

The Windsor Estate, Worthing (4)

Sixthly. Nor do any other thing that will derogate from the character which it is intended the whole of the said hereditaments shall bear or that will be a nuisance or annoyance to the neighbourhood.

And 7thly That the owner will assent to an apportionment of the tithe rent-charge and in the meanwhile will pay a proportion of the tithe rent-charge accordingly.

And whereas the idea of building on the said land so as aforesaid entertained 27 years ago has not yet been carried out, no building having been erected and the parties hereto desire to modify the covenants restricting the said land in manner hereinafter appearing –

Now this Indenture Witnesseth that the parties hereto do hereby severally covenant (the parties hereto of the 6th part covenanting as one) with each of the other parties hereto (the parties of the 6th part being one) so as to bind the owner or owners for the time being of the said Windsor Estate & every part thereof but not so as to make any person or persons responsible in respect of any breach committed after he or they shall have ceased to be the owner or owners of the same or of the part thereof upon or in respect of which such breach shall have been committed –

1. That the covenants hereinbefore referred to are to be construed as if the building lines therein mentioned were respectively ___ feet from Brighton Road, ___ feet from Church Walk and ___ feet from Windsor Rd but that as to the height of the fences and otherwise the said covenants remain unaltered.

Please suggest 11ft + 8.

2. That no house shall have a frontage of less than 20 feet but need not be detached or semidetached.

3.

Draft Deed modifying the Covenant 1902 (continued).

The Windsor Estate, Worthing (5)

> 3. That the sum of £   shall be substituted for £600 as the value of each house.
> 4. That the covenants against business excepting certain professions shall remain unaltered.
> 5. That the covenants against visible clothes or the burning of bricks or weeds shall remain unaltered.
> 6. The covenant not to do anything to derogate from the character of the neighbourhood shall: mean the character of the neighbourhood as modified by these presents.
> 7. The covenants as to tithe rent charge have been performed & the tithe rent charge redeemed.
>
> In Witness &c.
>
> **The Schedule**
>
> | | |
> |---|---|
> | Geo Jonathan Mills | Lots 16. 17. 18. 19. |
> | Edward C. Patching | Lot 15. |
> | John Butt & George W. Butt | Lots 11. 12. 13. 14. |
> | George Edwin Stone | Lots 9. 10. |
> | John Barnett | Lots 7. 8. |
> | Edwin Lephard, Robert Piper & Wm Edmund Wenban Smith | Lot 6. |
> | Melvill Green | Lots 1. 2. 3. 4. 5. |

Draft Deed modifying the Covenant 1902 (continued).

Appendix - item 1 - The Windsor Estate

The Windsor Estate, Worthing (6)

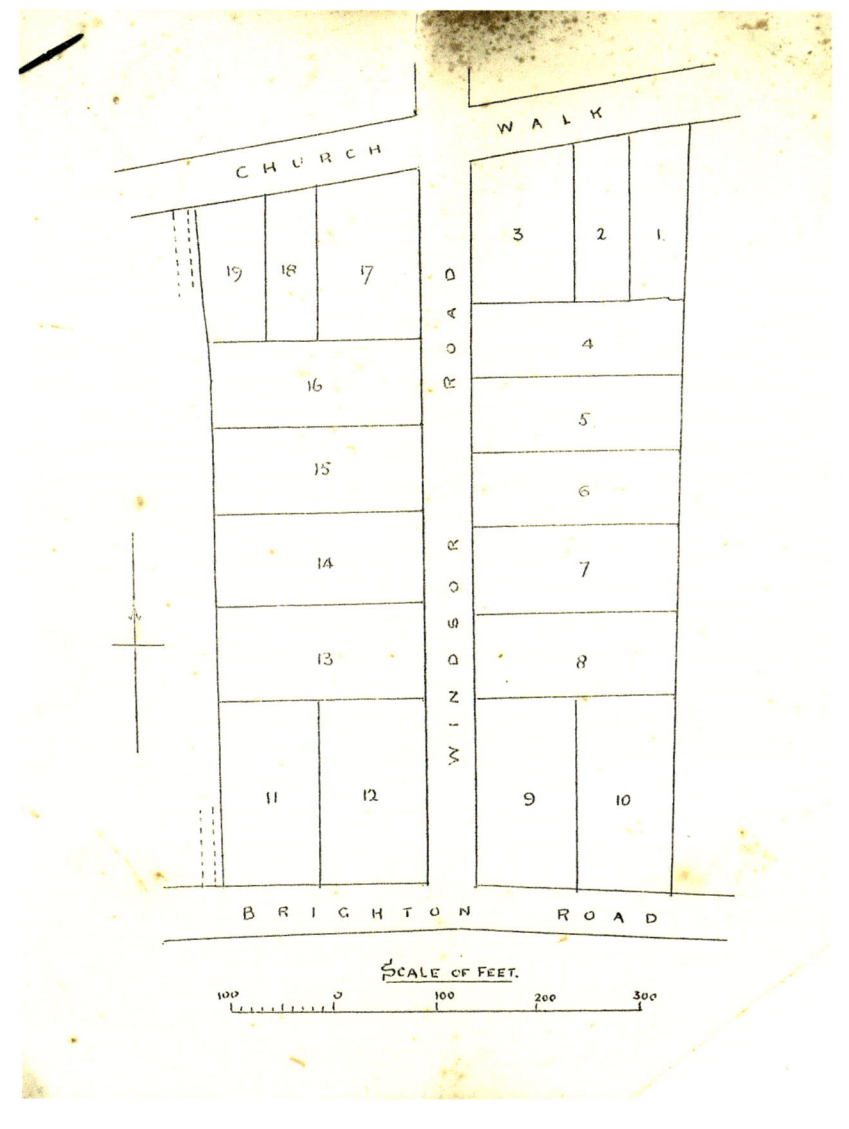

Draft Deed modifying the Covenant 1902 (continued).

Appendix - item 2 - Family Tree

Family Tree

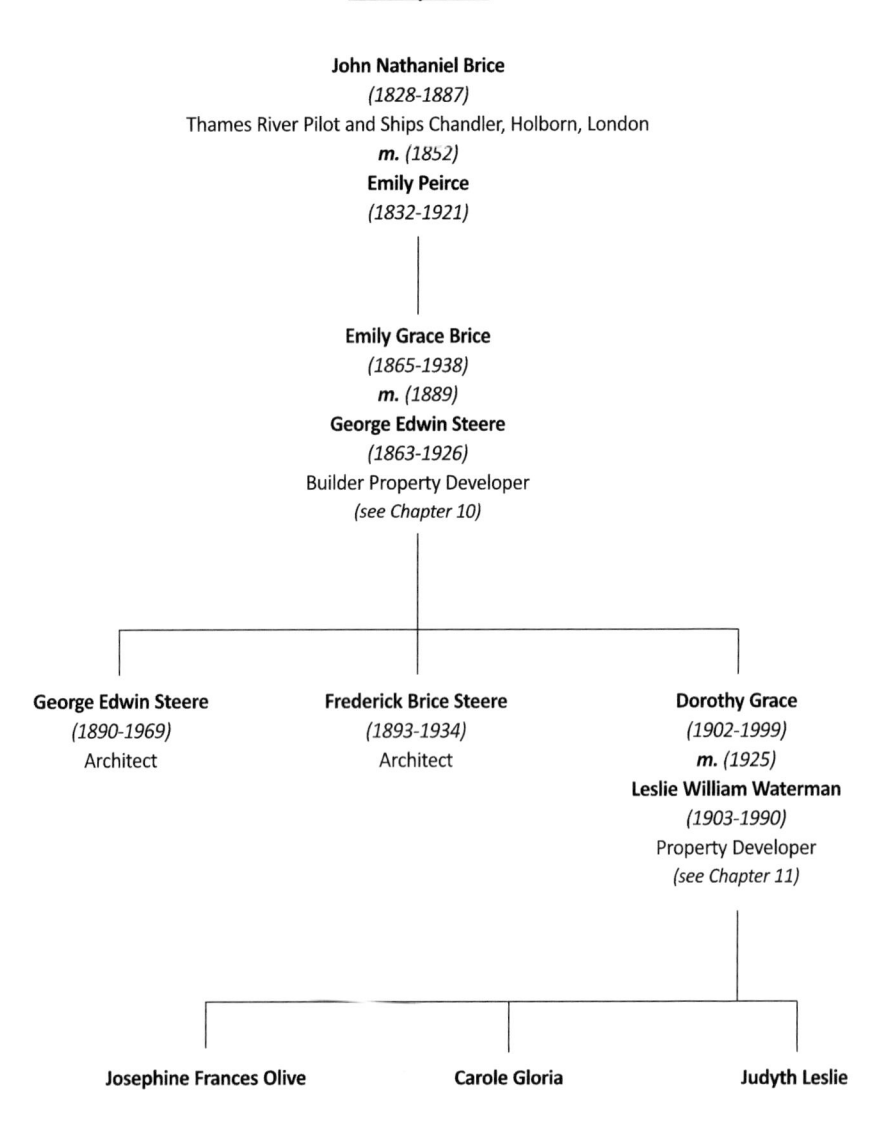

John Nathaniel Brice
(1828-1887)
Thames River Pilot and Ships Chandler, Holborn, London
***m.** (1852)*
Emily Peirce
(1832-1921)

Emily Grace Brice
(1865-1938)
***m.** (1889)*
George Edwin Steere
(1863-1926)
Builder Property Developer
(see Chapter 10)

George Edwin Steere	**Frederick Brice Steere**	**Dorothy Grace**
(1890-1969)	*(1893-1934)*	*(1902-1999)*
Architect	Architect	***m.** (1925)*
		Leslie William Waterman
		(1903-1990)
		Property Developer
		(see Chapter 11)

Josephine Frances Olive	**Carole Gloria**	**Judyth Leslie**

List of Buildings (1936)

Address of Property	Buildings
Clavadel, Downview Court, Boundary Road, (Downview Road), Worthing	36 Flats
Onslow Court, Brighton Road, East Worthing	30 Flats, 12 Garages
Broadmark Lane, Rustington	9 Flats over Shops
Bruce Avenue, Worthing	5 Houses
Clarence Court, Brighton Road (The Esplanade), East Worthing	Flats
Colonnade House (YCMA) Warwick Street, Worthing	-
George V Avenue, Worthing, Nos. 4-11	11 Houses
Goring Road Nos. 28,30,34,36,40,46,48,50,52,54,56,58,60,62,66 (Barclays Bank)	Shopping Centre
Goring Road Garages at the rear of Nos. 28,30,34,36,48,50	-
Grand Avenue Nos. 3,4,5, Hove	89 Flats
Winchester Court, Heene Road, West Worthing	12 Flats
Heene Way	12 Houses
Lancaster Court, Hurst Avenue, West Worthing	16 Flats
Mill Nursery, Lansdowne Road, Worthing	48 Flats
Liverpool Gardens No. 13, West Worthing	Office Block
Old Black Lion, Patcham	Land?
Park Drive, Rustington	4 Semi-detached Houses with Garages
Priory Dene, Rustington	House
St Winifrede's Road, Littlehampton	4 Houses
Thomas a Becket Development	Shopping Centre
Wellesley Court, Corner of Wallace Avenue and West Parade	12 Flats
West Parade Nos. 47,50, Worthing	4 Houses
Hastings Court, Winchelsea Gardens, Worthing	2 Blocks/Houses
Winchelsea Gardens, Block A,B,C, Worthing	66 Flats

Designed by known Architects.

Population and Houses Graph

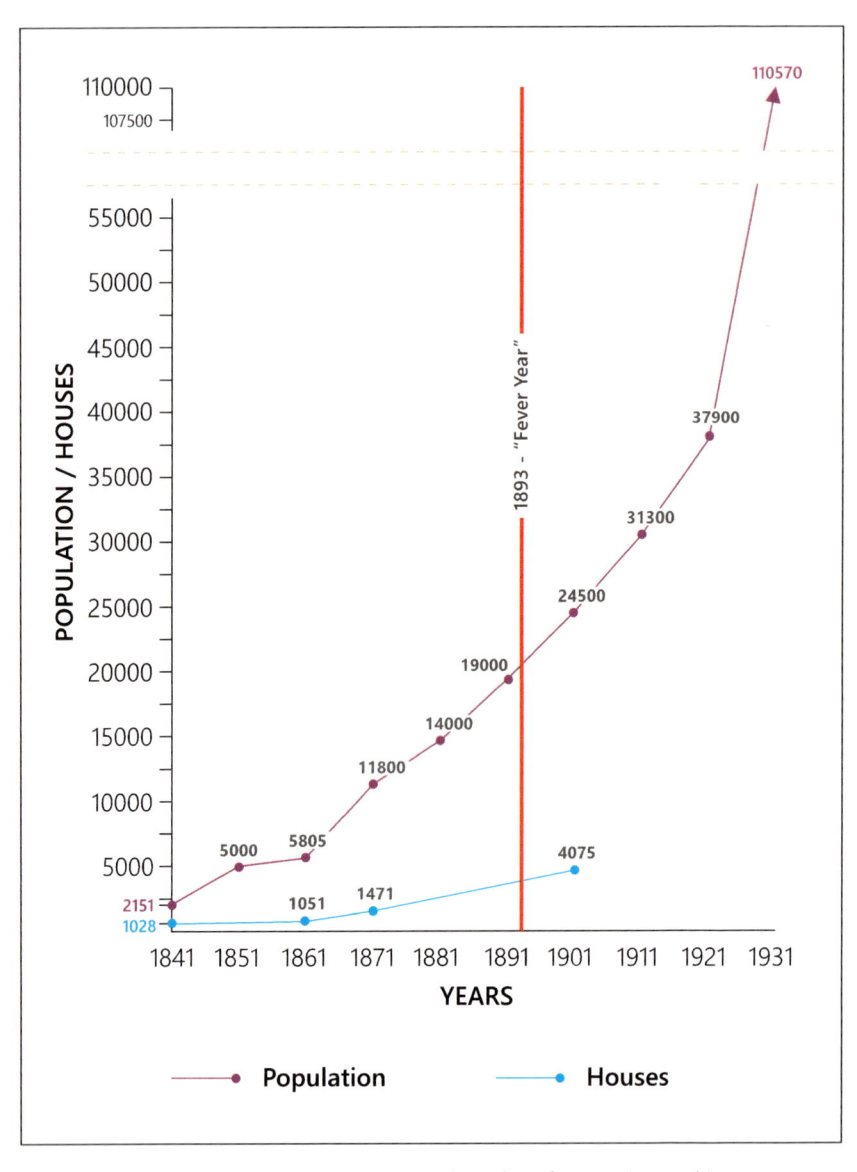

Year	Population	Houses
1841	2151	1028
1851	5000	1051
1861	5805	1051
1871	11800	1471
1881	14000	
1891	19000	
1901	24500	4075
1911	31300	
1921	37900	
1931	110570	

1893 - "Fever Year"

A graph showing the Population and number of Houses in Worthing from the period 1841-1931.

Appendix - item 5 - Maps

Map of Worthing Town Centre (1975)

Reproduced by kind permission of Alan Godfrey Maps.

Appendix - item 5 - Maps

Map of the River Adur (Sea Port)

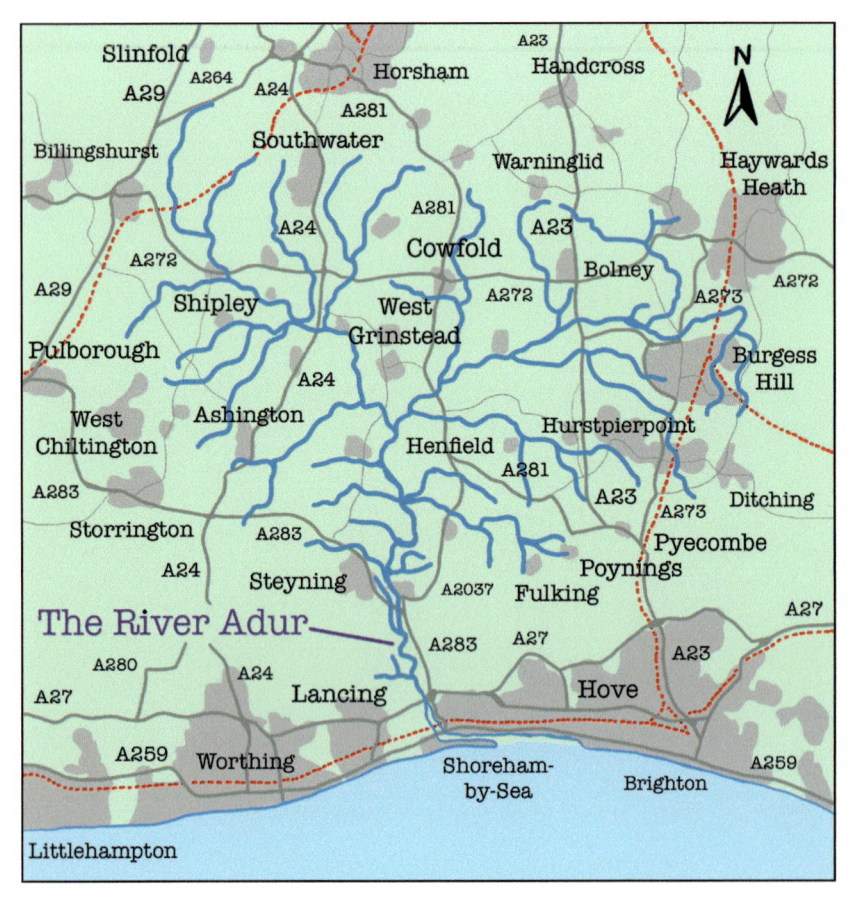

Recreated from an original by kind permission of Adur & Worthing Councils.

Appendix - item 5 - Maps

Map of the Brick Fields of Worthing

This map was taken from the Ordnance Survey Map of 1898.
Reproduced by kind permission of Alan Godfrey Maps.

Appendix - item 5 - Maps

Map of Worthing Districts (Wards)

Recreated from original illustration by kind permission of Ordnance Survey.

Architects and Eras

Victorian Era
1837-1901
Architectural Style - Medieval Gothic

Architect / Builder	**Decimus Burton 1800-1881** St Mary's Church, Goring 1836-1838
Architect / Builder	**John Biagio Rebecca 1800-1847** Beach House, Worthing Highdown House, Worthing Castle Goring, Worthing Buckingham Place, Shoreham Sea House Hotel, Worthing York Terrace, Worthing
Architect	**R C Carpenter 1812-1855** Lancing College
Civil Engineer	**Sir Robert Rawlinson 1810-1898** Worthing Pier
Architect / Civil Engineer	**G A Dean 1813/14-1898** Worthing Swimming Baths at Heene (Venetian Gothic) The Burlington Hotel, Marine Parade, Worthing The Downview Hotel, Worthing

Architects and Eras

Edwardian Era
1901-1910

Architectural Style - Art Nouveau 1880-1920

Architect / Builder **Stanley Davenport Adshead 1868-1946**

Architect / Builder **Stanley Churchill Ramsey 1882-1968**
The Worthing Concert Pavilion and Bandstand

Architect **George Edwin Steere 1880-1969**
and his brother
Frederick Steere (Brice) 1893-1934
Jointly and severally were responsible for designing their Mother's house 'Cliff Corner' at Lancing, and their own bungalows 'Taliaferro' (named after a flying field in Texas) and 'Tahoe' in Kings Road (formerly Farmers Lane), Lancing, both built in the style of Art Nouveau with hand crafted wood door latches etc. Their father was the builder/developer George Edwin Steere (see Chapter 10).

Architects and Eras

Modern Era including 'Art Deco' 1908-1935

Architect **Marcus Rainsford Fletcher 1907-1990**
Goring Shopping Centre, Worthing St.
Thomas A Becket Shopping Centre
(Tudor Revival)
Wellesley Court, West Worthing
Clarence Court, Worthing
Downview Court, Worthing

Architect **Arthur Thomas William Goldsmith 1892-1972**
and partner
Bernard Field Pennells
with offices at 13 Liverpool Gardens, Worthing
Heene Way
Onslow Court, Worthing 1934
Connaught Theatre in Art Deco style 1935
(previously the Picture Dome)

Modernism Era 1930's

Architect / Worthing Borough Engineer / Builder **Charles Hugh Wallis 1892-1941**
Five Green Pan-tile roofed houses on Brighton Road, Worthing

There were of course many other Architects working in and around the Worthing area during this time but the writer has been unable to trace either their name or specific areas of their work. It should be noted however that large firms such as Wood & Kendrick were also brought in alongside the local Architects.

Significant Dates in the Period 1853-1945

1853-1856   Crimean War

George Edwin Steere 1863-1926
1880-1881   First Boer War

1893   Fever in Worthing when 188 died from a typhoid outbreak with 1,300 catching the disease in a five-month period.

1899-1902   Second Boer War

1901   Coronation of Edward VII

Leslie William Waterman 1903-1990
1910-1936   King George V

1914-1918   World War I

1929   Wall Street Crash

1930's   'Great Depression'

1936-1952   King George VI

1939-1945   World War II

Appendix - item 8 - Rob Blann Newspaper Articles

Rob Blann Newspaper Article (1)

Family makes its mark on the town with development

TWO GENERATIONS of a Worthing family, both developers, between them built quite a large slice of Worthing: both the father and the first husband of 92-year-old Mrs Dorothy Cauchi (nee Steere), who wrote in with some stark revelations of the property world in days gone by.

It was her father, George Edwin Steere, who developed a substantial portion of South Broadwater, including most of Eastcourt Road, Westcourt Road and some of Northcourt Road as well as building several houses in nearby Bridge Road.

Speculation

South of the railway line, he put up a terrace of shops in Tarring Road to the east of the junction with Heene Road; the latter received his attention too when he arranged for several houses to be erected there.

At East Worthing he left his mark by constructing large seafront houses, mostly hotels, in Brighton Road, many of which later became hotels such as the Ingleside, the Anchorage and the Wolsey. Many other houses he built close-by in Navarino and Windsor Roads.

A stone's throw from there stands an Art Deco block of flats – Clarence Court – built by another of Dorothy's family, her first husband in fact, Leslie William Waterman.

Waterman's first speculation involved the purchase of a plot of land just north of Tarring village, part of an old apple orchard in what later became Rectory Road. The vendor, a chap by the name of Bashford, retained a section at the back and worked it as a market garden.

Waterman built two bungalows there on the west side of the road, the first was for Dorothy and became her first home as a married woman: "It cost £500 and we called it Apple Tree Cottage. Nice but small, later we added a sun parlour, opening from the sitting room. We made the garden, and one cold January day, before we took up

Remember When
By Rob Blann

residence, we both planted 100 or more fuschia cuttings all along the hedge separating our bungalow from the one next door called Chantry Cottage, which my husband also built.

"The builders themselves were rather rough types from Rochester but they knew their job, and while they did the work, camped in what was then a field opposite, now occupied by houses, one of which was built for Tom Kinch (of Kinch and Lack outfitters) and his wife Marjorie.

'Astonishing'

"In my little bungalow in Rectory Road I would cycle further down the street to a small grocer's, situated just about where the 'new' bit of road joins the 'old' one, leading to the old timbered houses. Our hastily planted fuschia hedge all grew, to my great surprise, and the wall of purple and crimson blossom was really an astonishing sight. I hope it is still there. The cuttings had been given to me by my father-in-law Edward Charles Waterman, who was on the town council for a number of years."

Having benefitted from the experience of building two properties in Rectory Road, her husband, at the young age of 26, left the employment of Patching's where he had been working in the estate office and embarked on a career as a developer by forming a company to build a series of houses and flats.

Next week we will discover which parts of Worthing they were responsible for constructing, and follow the rise and fall of that speculative property company, before tracing Dorothy's family in the aftermath of the company's collapse.

Copyright Rob Blann, 1995

Do you have an old photo or picture postcard tucked away? Or perhaps you have an interesting tale of bygone days? If so, please contact Rob Blann, 349 Tarring Road, Worthing BN11 5JL

A local historian, he has produced three fascinating books – A Town's Pride (£9.95) Edwardian Worthing (£12.95), and Worthing In Old Picture Postcards (£9.95) – all available from the author

AND NOW ON VIDEO: GLIMPSES OF PRE-WAR WORTHING AND EVERYDAY FOLK just £13.50 from Rob Blann.

Also, Mr Blann runs his own garden services business (see advert in page 24).

This article by Rob Blann appeared in the West Sussex Gazette, 26th January, 1995.

The Houses That George and William Built - Their Life & Times   113

Appendix - Item 8 - Rob Blann Newspaper Articles

Rob Blann Newspaper Article (2)

Family goes from riches to rags as the business folds

WHEN the speculative 1930s business masterminded by her first husband Leslie William Waterman untimely folded, causing terrible problems, Mrs Dorothy Cauchi succeeded in raising her children through the rough times.

After his first sucessful project building two bungalows on a Tarring orchard, detailed in last week's episode, Watermen left Patching's where he had been employed in the estate office and set about forming his own company.

He took on a builder as partner, a man by the name of George Victor Jeffery. "Registered as Jeffery

Remember When
by Rob Blann

Houses the company took offices in Chapel Road, on the corner of Chatsworth Road, just above the office of an old solicitor called Bennett," said Dorothy. Shortly after the company got underway another builder, Vincent Abel, joined the company.

The company developed more land in the parish of Tarring: Terringes Avenue, which they named after the ancient designation for Tarring, and also the older part of Ringmer Road.

They built more houses at various sites around Worthing: some in Rose Walk, Goring, designed by Marcus Fletcher; others along the Findon Road, the last bordering on the entrance to Bost Hill; as well as those in Heene Way, one of which was occupied by Dorothy and her husband for a while.

Jeffery Houses also built the mock Tudor shops on the corner of Goring Road and Elm grove.

The company erected the three Art Deco blocks of flats adorning Worthing's seafront: Wellesley Court at West Worthing on the corner of Wallace Avenue; Clarence Court at East Worthing on the corner of Marcus Fletcher; and Onslow Court in Brougham Road, designed by Arthur Goldsmith.

Still on the seafront road and just west of Brougham Road stand some green pan-tile roofed houses. These were also built by the company, using architect Hugh Wallis, who occupied one of them.

Under the management of Dorothy's husband, Leslie Waterman, Jeffery Houses flourished and expanded into a large and profitable business. "Although a clever man, he was a very bad judge of character," said Dorothy. Something went seriously wrong! The upshot of the whole sorry affair was that Jeffery Houses were put in the hands of the Receiver and

bankrupt.

"I never could find out the actual cause of the collapse," declared Dorothy, "but I do know my husband would not take part in any shady or criminal financial dealings, but he could be duped by very clever people, especially of high social standing and wealth. I never discovered the whole story, for I had my hands full trying to feed three children, nurse a sick husband after an appendix operation and then a breakdown, while rearing a one year-old baby."

The family retreated to a wooden shack she owned on the North Devon coast, politely called The Bungalow, a very basic place at the top of the beach where "we lived like gipsies, ate the plainest food, survived and by way of compensation had excellent health."

Those days must have stood her in good stead, for even now at the age of 92 she is still in reasonable health!

■ I have received the following letter from Alan Randall, Chief Executive of Worthing and Southlands Hospitals: "I just wanted you to know how I enjoyed your piece about Roy Affleck (WSG, January 19). It has been my good fortune to work with him since 1983. His sharp sense of humour and his strong Socialist views have always been in evidence. He has been a good friend and supporter of the hospital and the local NHS. I was very sorry when he recently became ill and miss our regular meetings. Reading his life story was fascinating and very enjoyable."

Copyright Rob Blann, 1995
Do you have an old photo or picture postcard tucked away? Or perhaps you have an interesting tale of bygone days? If so, please contact Rob Blann, 349 Tarring Road, Worthing BN11 5JL.

A local historian, he has produced three fascinating books – A Town's Pride (£9.95), Edwardian Worthing (£12.95), and Worthing In Old Picture Postcards (£9.95) – all available from the author.

AND NOW ON VIDEO: GLIMPSES OF PRE-WAR WORTHING AND EVERYDAY FOLK just £13.50 from Rob Blann.

Also, Mr Blann runs his own garden services business (see advert in page 24).

100 Years Ago

(From the WSG of January 31, 1895).
WORTHING - Four youths, named William Fielder, George Cobby, Frank Dawson, and William Virgoe, were summoned for trespassing on land belonging to Mr H.A. Jee, Sompting, on Sunday last, in search of rabbits. Evidence was given by PC Cobb and PC Woodland, who saw defendants on Sunday last for nearly four hours hunting the hedge rows in the brook lands at the Decoy. Fielder was caught he had a recently killed rabbit tucked inside his trousers. The defendants denied they were searching for rabbits, and asserted that they only went there for a slide. Previous convictions were proved against Dawson, Virgoe and Cobby. Fielder was fined 2s 6d and 6s costs or five days; Cobby 5s and costs 6s, or seven days; Dawson 7s 6d and 6s costs, or ten days; Virgoe 5s and costs 6s, or seven days.

50 Years Ago

(From the WSG of February 1, 1945).
HORSHAM - A very welcome respite has come to members of the Special Constabulary. For the first time since the summer of 1939 they have been "stood down" from their patrol duties and, it is understood, will not be called upon except in the case of emergency. Generous public acknowledgement of the value of their services is due to these men - many of whom did long hours of black-out duty after a full day of civil employment, some of them approaching 70 years of age.

This article by Rob Blann, appeared in the West Sussex Gazette, February, 1995.

Appendix - item 9 - Before Clarence Court

Before Clarence Court was built. Looking westward from the beach at East Worthing, this 1912 view shows large houses on the right in Brighton Road built by Dorothy's father.

The Houses That George and William Built - Their Life & Times

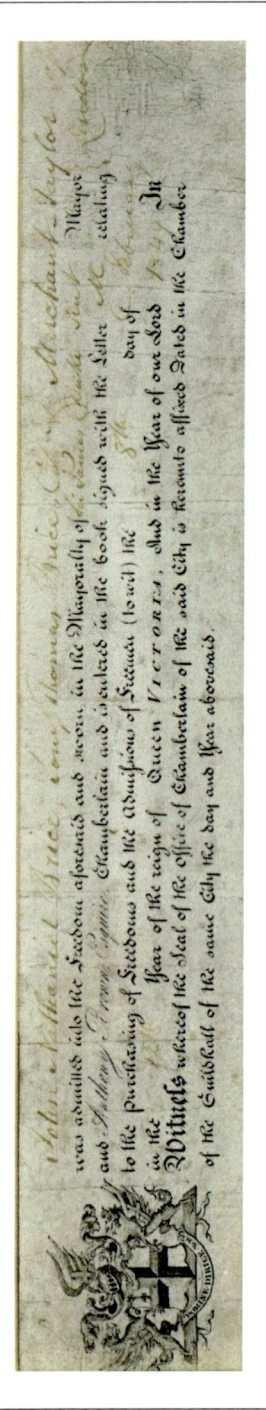

Appendix - item 10 - Freedom of the City of London

John Nathaniel Brice Copy of the Document - Freedom of the City of London, dated 1849.
Due to the age of this document and the fading of the text I give the wording in full below:

John Nathaniel Brice, Son of Thomas Brice, Currently a Merchant Taylor of London was admitted into the Freedom aforesaid and sworn in the Mayoralty of Sir James Clarke First Mayor and Anthony Brown Esquire, Chamberlain and is entered in the book signed with the Letter M relating to the purchasing of Freedoms and Admissions of Freemen (to wit) the 8th day of February in the 12th Year of the reign of Queen VICTORIA, and in the Year of our Lord 1849. In Witness whereof the Seal of the Office of Chamberlain of the said City is hereunto affixed Dated in the Chamber of the Guildhall of the same City the day and Year aboveseid.

Acknowledgements

Susan Belton, The Worthing Society Chair
Rob Blann
Miss Nina Durrant
Chris Green (The Walking Historian)
Anthony Gwynne
Catherine Gwynne
Susan Gwynne
Josephine Jones
Saville Jones, Architect
John Lifford
Lorraine Manchester (photographs)
David Martin, Martin Group Services
Paul Martin, Redsmart
Rosemary Pearson and Friends of Broadwater and Worthing Cemetery
Florence Pillman, London (Research V & A Theatre)
Royal Society of British Architects
Kitty Shepherd, (Onslow Court Tenants Association)
    who kindly supplied the Brochure and other material relating to
    Onslow Court
Carole Sinclair
Jessica Toomey
Martin C.B. Toomey
Sam White, Worthing Reference Library
Sue Worrall, Librarian Crawley Library, West Sussex County Council
Worthing Library, Richmond Road
Worthing Museum & Art Gallery

Additional to the above list of those who have helped me to write this book a special mention should be made of my Secretary, Researcher and Friend, Samantha Kendrick who over the past four years has seen the highs and lows of this developing and intriguing story of my family.

Index of Names

A Becket Gardens - Chapter 8
Adshead Stanley Davenport - See List of Architects and Eras
Anchorage Hotel - Chapter 10
Antarctic - Chapters 1 and 6
Apple Tree Cottage - Chapters 1 and 11
Arun - Chapter 5
Ashington - Chapter 5
Austin 1922 Tourer - Chapter 7
Baltimore Guest House - Chapter 10
Barclays Bank - Chapters 8 and 11
Bathing Machines (Chariots) - Chapter 2
Battye Deryk (Cyril) - Chapter 4
Battye Evelyn Désireé - Chapter 4
Battye Montague - Chapter 4
Beach House Gardens - Chapter 6
Beeding Portland Cement Co - Chapter 1
Beeton Mrs - Chapter 8
Billingsgate Market - Chapters 9 and 10
Bishops Stortford - Chapter 11
Blaker Mr - Chapter 10
Blann Charlotte Susan - Chapters 9 and 10
Blann Rob - Chapter 11
Bostal The - Chapter 5
Bournville - Chapter 1
Bow Street Runners - Chapter 5
Brennan Margaret - Chapters 4 and 10
Brice Emily Grace (Steere) - Chapters 5 and 10
Brice John (Jack) - Chapter 10
Brice John Nathaniel - Chapter 10
Bridge Road - Chapter 10
Brighton - Chapters 2, 4, 7 and 11
Brighton College of Technology - Chapter 11

Index of Names

Brighton Road - Chapters 8, 9 and 10
Broadwater - Chapters 4, 9 and 10
Broadwater Cemetery - Chapter 10
Broadwater Church - Chapter 4
Bulkington Avenue - Chapter 6
Burton Decimus - See List of Architects and Eras
Cadbury George - Chapter 1
Canadian Army - Chapter 8
Carlton Colville - Chapter 9
Carpenter R C - See List of Architects and Eras
Carter Charlotte - Chapter 4
Carter Kate - Chapter 4
Cassels Bertha Lady - Chapters 5 ,6, and 7
Cassels Frank - Chapters 4 and 7
Cassels Ronnie - Chapters 4 and 7
Cassels Sir James - Chapters 1, 6 and 7
Chanctonbury Ring - Chapters 1, 5 and 10
Chantry Cottage - Chapters 1 and 11
Cissbury Ring - Chapter 4
Clapham Woods - Chapter 5
Clarence Court - Chapters 8 and 11
Coast Kate - Chapter 6
Cocozzer Mr - Chapter 2
Coe Mr - Chapter 2
Coley Henry - Chapter 5
Colonnade House - Chapter 8
Colville, 33 Gratwicke Road - Chapter 9
Cresy Edward - Chapter 2
Daimler - Chapter 7
Dean G A - See List of Architects and Eras
Decoy Lane - Chapter 4
Downview Court - Chapter 8
Durrington Cemetery - Chapter 11
Earth Closets - Chapter 2
Eastcourt Road - Chapters 9 and 10

Index of Names

Ferrari Guido - Chapter 2
Field Lodge - Chapter 10
Fields W C - Chapter 4
Fittleworth - Chapter 5
Fletcher Marcus Rainsford - Chapters 8 and 11
Freedom of the City of London Document - Chapter 10
Freeman William - Chapter 9
Gavin Alex - Chapter 6
George V Avenue - Chapter 10
Girl's Secondary School - Chapter 6
Goldsmith Arthur Thomas William - Chapter 8
Goring - Chapter 10
Goring-by-Sea - Chapter 2
Goring Road - Chapters 8 and 11
Grand Avenue - Chapter 4
Gray's Inn Gardens - Chapter 10
Half Brick Public House - Chapter 5
Ham Road - Chapter 4
Harrison Nielia - Chapter 3
Hassocks - Chapter 1
Hastings - Chapter 9
Hawich Mr - Chapter 7
Heathcote John - Chapter 7
Heene - Chapter 9
Heene Cemetery - Chapter 9
Heene Estate Company - Chapter 10
Heene Road - Chapter 10
Heene Way - Chapters 1 and 8
Highdown - Chapter 5
The High School - Chapter 6
Holborn - Chapter 10
Horse bus - Chapter 7
Howard Sir Ebenezer - Chapter 1
Indian Motorcycle - Chapter 7
Ingleside Hotel - Chapter 10

Index of Names

James 750 Motorcycle - Chapter 7
Jeffery & Co - Chapter 11
Jeffery George Victor - Chapter 11
Jeffery Houses - Chapter 11
Jones Josephine - Chapters 8 and 11
Jowett - Chapter 7
King George VI - Chapter 11
Knickerbocker suits - Chapter 3
Knight Templars - Chapter 4
Kursall (Dome) - Chapter 3
Lalla Rouke - Chapter 7
Lancaster Court - Chapter 8
Lancing - Chapters 1, 7 and 10
Lavender Fields - Chapter 11
Lephard & Paine - Chapter 9
Lephard Edwin - Chapter 9
Lever William - Chapter 1
Littlehampton - Chapter 5
Littlehampton Road - Chapters 8 and 11
Loudon John Claudius - Chapter 10
Lowestoft - Chapter 9
Mace Jim - Chapter 6
Matley Ada - Chapters 7 and 11
Matley Frank - Chapters 7 and 11
Miller's Grove - Chapter 5
Mills George Jonathan - Chapters 9 and 10
Montague Street - Chapters 2 and 4
Motorcycle James 750 - Chapter 7
Mount Carvey - Chapter 4
Mowlems - Chapter 11
Navarino Road - Chapter 10
New Town, Worthing - Chapter 10
Newich (Newick) - Chapter 5
Norfolk Duke of - Chapter 9
Northcourt Road - Chapter 10

Index of Names

Offington Park - Chapter 1
Old Salts Farm Lane - Chapter 1
Onslow Court - Chapter 8
Paine George - Chapter 9
Pantiles - Chapter 8
Pattern Books - Chapters 8 and 10
Patterns (Pattens) - Chapter 5
Peirce Emily - Chapter 10
Peirce Sarah - Chapters 2 and 5
Pennells Bernard Field - See List of Architects and Eras
Peter Robinson of Oxford Street - Chapters 4 and 10
"Plus Fours" - Chapter 3
Port Sunlight - Chapter 1
Pulborough - Chapters 5 and 7
Queen Victoria - Chapter 6
Ramsey Stanley Davenport - See List of Architects and Eras
Rawlinson Sir Robert - See List of Architects and Eras
Rebecca John Biagio - See List of Architects and Eras
Richards Frank - Chapter 4
Richardson William Westbrooke - Chapter 10
Riches Georgiana (Mills) - Chapter 9
Robinson Lucy - Chapter 6
Rochdale - Chapter 1
Russell Dr Richard - Chapter 2
Salt Titus - Chapter 1
Saltaire - Chapter 1
Saville Jones - Chapter 8
Scott Captain - Chapter 6
Seamills Bridge - Chapter 2
Shoreham - Chapters 1 and 10
Simpson Dr - Chapter 7
Smith & Strange - Chapter 1
Smithfield - Chapter 7
Sompting - Chapter 4
South Farm - Chapter 6

Index of Names

Southcourt Road - Chapter 10
Southdown Motor Services - Chapter 7
Southwick - Chapter 4
Spanish 'Flu' - Chapter 11
St Thomas a Becket - Chapters 8 and 11
Stanley Mr & Mrs - Chapter 4
Steam Lorries (Wagons) - Chapter 1
Steere Dorothy Grace - All Chapters except chapter 8
Steere Dorothy May - Chapters 9 and 10
Steere Emily (Brice) - Chapter 10
Steere Frederick Brice - Chapters 2 and 10
Steere George - Chapters 2 and 10
Steere George Carter - Chapter 10
Steere George Edwin - Chapters 1, 2, 6, 8, 9, 10 and 11
Steyne School - Chapters 6 and 7
Storrington - Chapter 5
Strange Joan - Chapters 1 and 6
Strange Kitty - Chapters 1 and 6
Strange Mr - Chapter 1
'Sundial' - Chapters 1 and 4
Swan Inn The, Fittleworth - Chapter 5
Symond Gladys - Chapter 2
Symond Horace - Chapter 2
Tarring Estate - Chapter 8
Tarring Road - Chapter 10
Tarring Village - Chapter 11
Terry Alfred - Chapter 7
Terry Lucy - Chapter 5
Teville Road - Chapter 10
Teville Stream - Chapter 10
Theatre Royal, Bath Place - Chapter 4
Tram-O-Cars - Chapter 7
Vicarage Road - Chapter 10
Wallace Nellie - Chapter 4

Index of Names

Wallis Charles Hugh - Chapter 8
Wallis Olive - Chapter 8
Warwick House Estate - Chapter 2
Washington - Chapter 2
Washington Farm - Chapter 7
Waterman Edward Charles - Chapters 2 and 11
Waterman Ernest - Chapters 10 and 11
Waterman Leslie William - Chapters 8, 10 and 11
Wellesley Court - Chapter 8
West Sussex Constabulary - Chapter 5
West Sussex Gazette - Chapter 11
West Worthing Estate - Chapter 2
West Worthing - Chapter 10
West Worthing Investment Company - Chapter 10
Westcourt Road - Chapter 10
Windsor Estate - Chapters 1, 9 and 10
Windsor Hotel - Chapter 10
Windsor Military Knights - Chapter 4
Windsor Road - Chapter 10
Winter Hall - Chapter 4
Wolsey Hotel - Chapter 10
Wood & Kendrick - Chapter 8
Worthing Motor Services - Chapter 7
Worthing Pier - Chapter 4
Worthing Record - Chapter 7
Worthing Typhoid Epidemic - Chapter 2
Worthing Water Works - Chapters 1 and 2
York Duke of - Chapter 11